D0874910

Cases and Controversies in U.S. History

by
J. Weston Walch
with
Kate O'Halloran

J. Weston Walch, Publisher
Portland, Maine

Users' Guide
to
Walch Reproducible Books

As part of our general effort to provide educational materials which are as practical and economical as possible, we have designated this publication a "reproducible book." The designation means that purchase of the book includes purchase of the right to limited reproduction of all pages on which this symbol appears:

Here is the basic Walch policy: We grant to individual purchasers of this book the right to make sufficient copies of reproducible pages for use by all students of a single teacher. This permission is limited to a single teacher, and does not apply to entire schools or school systems, so institutions purchasing the book should pass the permission on to a single teacher. Copying of the book or its parts for resale is prohibited.

Any questions regarding this policy or requests to purchase further reproduction rights should be addressed to:

Permissions Editor
J. Weston Walch, Publisher
P.O. Box 658
Portland, ME 04104-0658

—*J. Weston Walch, Publisher*

1   2   3   4   5   6   7   8   9   10

ISBN 0-8251-2320-8
Copyright © 1993
J. Weston Walch, Publisher
P.O. Box 658 • Portland, Maine 04104-0658

Printed in the United States of America

Contents

Introduction

A history teacher once asked a student, "What are the addresses we associate with Washington and Lincoln?" The boy replied, "Mount Vernon and Springfield." He had learned the facts of history, but knew nothing of its living words, its voice. And he is not alone. To many students, history is dead and dull. They see no relationship between the facts of the past and their own lives in the present. Their knowledge comes to them in the words of historians, not in the words of the people who watched history being made or the people who made it themselves.

In this book, we restore history's voice. We have gathered contemporary source documents, from a 12th-century Viking saga to recent Supreme Court cases, to introduce students to 50 cases and controversies in U.S. history. By studying original material, students are brought closer to the actual events and to the people who took part in them.

Here, then, is history in action. This is a very dramatic way to teach history, similar to the case method of teaching law. Using the case method, students get the facts, make their decision, and then compare their decision to the outcome of the case. In this book, each unit includes a brief introduction, a carefully selected excerpt from a critical source document, and questions to guide student reading and reaction.

Although this book does offer sample answers to most questions, there are no "right" and "wrong" answers. In keeping with an issues-centered approach to social studies, we have designed these questions to encourage your students to think about the issues and form their own opinions. Only a few questions require a knowledge of events not presented in the unit. This makes *Cases and Controversies in U.S. History* an ideal introduction to different periods of history. As students get involved in the issues, they want to know more about the events.

Many of the units in this book are also suitable for small group work. Students can work in groups to rewrite excerpts in their own words. Groups are also ideal for some of the "brainstorming" activities—thinking of arguments for or against a proposition, naming the possible effects of an event, etc. Many of the situations, particularly the ones based on actual law cases, can also be used to stage mock trials. Students play the parts of judge and jury, prosecution, defense, etc. If they wish, they can do further research for their roles, or they can improvise from the material provided on each case. (A brief suggested reading list is included in the teacher section of each unit.) Or you can divide the class into two teams and have each team present one side of an argument—for example, that instead of celebrating Columbus Day, we should celebrate Leif Eriksson Day.

Of course, using original source material may be quite a challenge for some students, particularly with some of the older excerpts. You might ask students to scan the passage first, to see if they can get an overall sense of the meaning before reading the details. You might want to go through the toughest readings with the class. Or you could break the class into groups of three or four and have each group work on an excerpt together. Several units ask students to rewrite part or all of the excerpt in their own words, either individually or as a group. With the more challenging documents, you might ask students to rewrite the excerpt as an introductory exercise. Most units include a brief glossary of problematic words for student use.

As they read the excerpts, ask students to keep some general questions in mind. To whom was the piece originally addressed? What was it intended to achieve? Is the student's own life affected in any way by what happened here? And how was the piece affected by time and circumstances—does the same idea reappear in different words at different periods of history, or were the ideas unique to a specific time? If students read with these things in mind, they will find the unit questions easier to answer.

Another general approach is to ask students why they think the material constitutes a "case" or a "controversy." What basic question comes to mind as they read each excerpt? Identifying the issue will help students focus with accuracy and understanding on the information. In most cases, more than one basic question can be found. We present one possibility at the beginning of the "Sample Answers" section of each unit.

Whether you use this book to introduce students to different periods or to stimulate discussion in the classroom, you will find it a useful tool for making your students part of history. And the more present they can feel in the events of the past, the more they will realize how the past affects the present, and the role history plays in all our lives.

For Further Reading—General

Adler, Mortimer, ed. *The Annals of America: Fourteen Ninety-Three to Nineteen Seventy-Three*, 23 vols. Chicago: Encyclopedia Britannica, 1976.

Aptheker, Herbert, ed. *A Documentary History of the Negro People in the United States*, 3 vols. Secaucus: Citadel Press, 1974.

Bailey, Thomas A. *The American Spirit: American History As Seen by Contemporaries*, 2 vols. (5th ed.). Indianapolis: Heath, 1984.

Brandon, William. *Indians*. New York: American Heritage, 1985.

Brown, Dee. *Bury My Heart at Wounded Knee: An American Indian History of the American West*. New York: Holt, Rinehart and Winston, 1970.

Commager, Henry Steele, ed. *Documents of American History*, 10th edition. Englewood Cliffs, NJ: Prentice-Hall, 1988.

Davis, Kenneth C. *Don't Know Much About History*. New York: Crown Publishers, Inc., 1990.

Evans, Sara M. *Born for Liberty: A History of Women in America*. New York: Free Press, 1989.

Heffner, Richard D. *A Documentary History of the United States*. New York: New American Library, 1985.

Hofstadter, Richard, and Clarence L. Ver Steeg. *Great Issues in American History*, 3 vols. New York: Vintage, 1958.

Morison, Samuel Eliot, ed. *Sources and Documents Illustrating the American Revolution, 1764-1788, and the Formation of the Federal Constitution*. New York: Oxford University Press, 1965.

National Archives and Records Administration and National Council for the Social Studies. *Teaching With Documents: Using Primary Sources from the National Archives*. Washington, D.C.: National Archives and Records Administration, 1989.

Vaughan, Alden T., ed. *Chronicles of the American Revolution*. New York: Grosset & Dunlap, 1965.

Zinn, Howard. *A People's History of the United States*. New York: Harper & Row, 1980.

1000—Leif Eriksson Explores Vinland

In 1963, a site yielding Viking artifacts was found on the northern tip of Newfoundland. It is now thought to be the site of the community established by Leif Eriksson and Thorfinn Karlsefni. Here is an excerpt from a Norse saga describing Leif's first voyage to the west.

They sailed away to sea in a north-east wind for two days until they sighted land again. They sailed towards it and came to an island which lay to the north of it.

They went ashore and looked about them. The weather was fine. There was dew on the grass, and the first thing they did was to get some of it on their hands and put it to their lips, and to them it seemed the sweetest thing they had ever tasted. Then they went back to their ship and sailed into the sound that lay between the island and the headland jutting out to the north.

They steered a westerly course round the headland. There were extensive shallows there and at low tide their ship was left high and dry, with the sea almost out of sight. . . . As soon as the tide had refloated the ship they took a boat and rowed out to it and brought it up the river into the lake, where they anchored it. They carried their hammocks ashore and put up booths. Then they decided to winter there, and built some large houses.

There was no lack of salmon in the river or the lake, bigger salmon than they had ever seen. The country seemed to them so kind that no winter fodder would be needed for livestock; there was never any frost all winter and the grass hardly withered at all.

In this country, night and day were of more even length than in either Greenland or Iceland: on the shortest day of the year, the sun was already up by 9 a.m., and did not set until after 3 p.m. [*The Graenlendinga Saga*, c. 1190]

——Questions——

1. What significance did this Viking settlement have in American history?

2. What information in this excerpt might help researchers locate the site of the Viking settlement?

3. Christopher Columbus is usually referred to as having "discovered" the American continent. But the continent was already settled by native Americans, and the Vikings were aware of America centuries before Columbus. Why is Columbus's voyage considered so important?

GLOSSARY   **artifact**—item made or worked by humans

Sample Answers
Leif Eriksson Explores Vinland

A Basic Question: How significant was this exploration?

1. The Viking discovery of America had no impact on the future course of American history. The settlement was abandoned, discouraged by the constant threat of attack by the natives, whom the Vikings called Skraelings.

2. The description of the weather is less helpful than it appears at first, as the world climate has changed dramatically in the last millennium. For this reason, the references to wildlife are also difficult to rely on, although, on the east coast of the North American continent, salmon are not usually found south of the Hudson River. However, the references to the amount of daylight can be used to approximate latitude. If the shortest days of the year were at least six hours long, then the location must be south of latitude fifty and north of latitude forty, or somewhere between the Gulf of St. Lawrence and New Jersey.

3. Although the Vikings were aware of America, they did not pursue their attempts to colonize the continent, and did little to share their knowledge with other people. Columbus's voyage was the one which, for better or worse, let all Europe know of the existence of an unknown land to the west.

For Further Reading

Babcock, William H. *Early Norse Visits to North America.* New York: Gordon Press, 1976.

Chapman, Paul H. *The Norse Discovery of America.* Atlanta: One Candle Press, 1981.

Lauber, Patricia. *Who Discovered America.* New York: Random House, 1970.

Magnusson, Magnus, and Hermann Palsson. *The Vinland Sagas: The Norse Discovery of America.* New York: Penguin, 1965.

Quinn, David B. *North America from Earliest Discovery to First Settlement: The Norse Voyages to 1612.* New York: Harper & Row, 1977.

Reman, Edward. *The Norse Discoveries and Explorations in America.* Westport: Greenwood, 1976 (Reprint of 1949 edition).

1492—Privileges and Prerogatives Granted to Columbus

For years, Columbus had been trying to find someone to finance his idea. He wanted to sail westward to reach India. Finally King Ferdinand and Queen Isabella of Spain agreed to help him. Here is an excerpt from the terms they agreed to.

For as much of you, Christopher Columbus, are going by our command, with some of our vessels and men, to discover and subdue some islands and continent in the ocean, and it is hoped that by God's assistance, some of the said islands and continent in the ocean will be discovered and conquered by your means and conduct, therefore it is but just and reasonable, that since you expose yourself to such danger to serve us, you should be rewarded for it. And we being willing to honour and favour you for the reasons aforesaid; Our will is, that you, Christopher Columbus, after discovering and conquering the said islands and continent in the said ocean, or any of them, shall be our admiral of the said islands and continent you shall so discover and conquer; and that you be our admiral, viceroy, and governor in them, and that for the future, you may call and style yourself, D. Christopher Columbus, and that your sons and successors in the said employment, may call themselves dons, admirals, viceroys, and governors of them. [Privileges and Prerogatives Granted to Columbus, April 30, 1492]

——Questions——

1. Based on this passage, what do you think were Columbus's motives for sailing west?

2. One of the rewards Columbus was given was being allowed to call himself "D. Christopher Columbus." What do you think was the significance of this?

3. What were Ferdinand's and Isabella's motives in supporting him?

4. Why do you think some people see Columbus as a destroyer, not a discoverer?

GLOSSARY aforesaid—as mentioned earlier
don—Spanish nobleman

viceroy—governor who rules as representative of a king

Sample Answers
Privileges and Prerogatives Granted to Columbus

A Basic Question: Was Columbus more discoverer or destroyer?

1. Columbus was looking for personal gain. In the passage quoted, Isabella and Ferdinand promise to reward Columbus if he discovers any new countries for them. In fact, negotiations with Ferdinand and Isabella were broken off earlier, as the terms Columbus was setting were considered exorbitant.

2. The "D" stands for Don, which was a title used by Spanish nobles. The king and queen are saying here that Columbus, an Italian adventurer, will now be considered a member of the Spanish nobility.

3. Isabella and Ferdinand were looking for an easier route to India. Spain had just driven out the Moorish forces, and now had the time and resources to look elsewhere for territory. The passage quoted makes it clear that the king and queen did not consider the possible wishes of the people living in the lands Columbus might find. They wanted him to "discover and subdue" territory, to increase the wealth of Spain.

4. People who argue that Columbus was a destroyer, not a discoverer, point out that when we talk about "discovering" America, we really mean "making America known to Europe." People had already been living in America for centuries. Many different civilizations and ways of life flourished in the continent. (It had even been "discovered" before by Europeans. In the early years of the eleventh century, there was a Viking settlement in Newfoundland.) But to Columbus and other European explorers, the newfound lands, and the people who lived in them, were there only to be exploited.

For Further Reading

Columbus, Christopher. *The Voyage of Christopher Columbus: Columbus' Own Journal of Discovery.* Cummins, John G., trans. New York: St. Martin's Press, 1992.

Morison, Samuel Eliot. *The Great Explorers.* New York: Oxford University Press, 1978.

1494—The Treaty of Tordesillas

After Columbus's discoveries in 1492, both Spain and Portugal were eager to explore further and claim more new lands. To prevent disagreements, they appealed to Pope Alexander VI. The pope drew an imaginary line from north to south, 100 leagues west of the Cape Verde Islands. Anything discovered west of that line would belong to Spain; anything east, to Portugal. However, King John of Portugal was not satisfied with these provisions. In the Treaty of Tordesillas, Spain and Portugal agreed to move the boundary line to 370 leagues west of the Cape Verde Islands.

This boundary or line shall be drawn straight, as aforesaid, at a distant of three hundred and seventy leagues west of the Cape Verde Islands. . . . And all lands, both islands and mainlands, found and discovered already, or to be found and discovered hereafter, by the said King of Portugal and his vessels on this side of the said line and bound determined as above, toward the east, in either north or south latitude, on the eastern side of the said bound, provided the said bound is not crossed, shall belong to and remain in the possession of, and pertain forever to, the said King of Portugal and his successors. And all other lands, both islands and mainlands, found or to be found hereafter, . . . by the said King and Queen of Castile, Aragon, etc. and by their vessels, on the western side of the said bound, determined as above, after having passed the said bound toward the west, in either its north or south latitude, shall belong to . . . the said King and Queen of Castile, Leon, etc. and to their successors. [The Treaty of Tordesillas, 1494]

——Questions——

1. In this treaty, Spain and Portugal divide the unknown world between them, assuming that any further discoveries will be made by Spanish and Portuguese explorers. Why do you think they made this assumption?

2. If you had been an English explorer, how would you have felt about this treaty?

3. What effect did the Treaty of Tordesillas have on the future of the American continent?

Glossary   **hereafter**—from now on
league—three miles

     Cases and Controversies in U.S. History

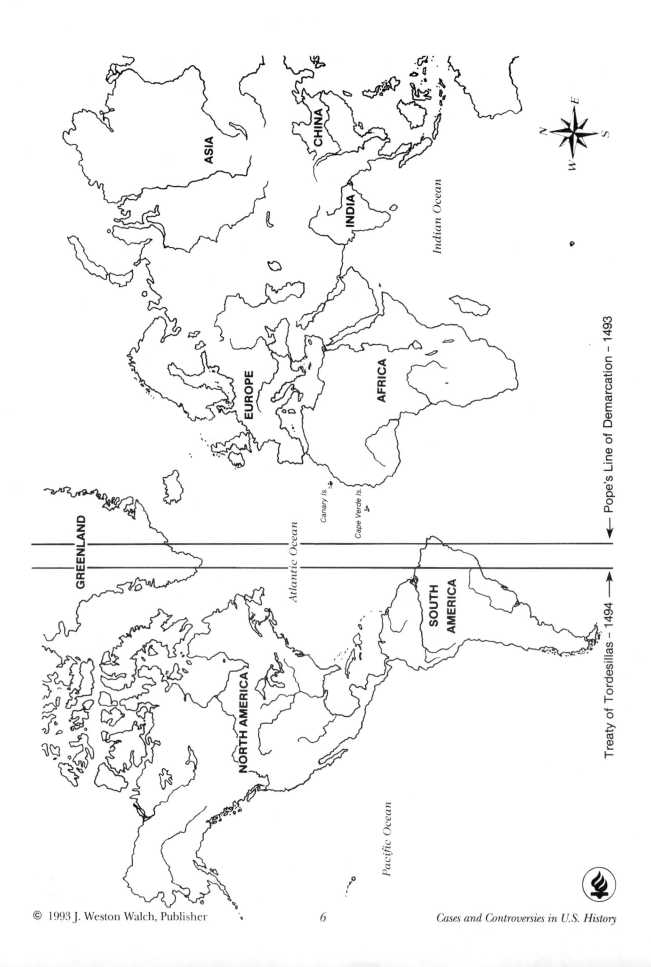

GREENLAND

NORTH AMERICA

SOUTH AMERICA

Atlantic Ocean

Pacific Ocean

Canary Is.

Cape Verde Is.

EUROPE

ASIA

CHINA

INDIA

AFRICA

Indian Ocean

Treaty of Tordesillas – 1494 →

← Pope's Line of Demarcation – 1493

Cases and Controversies in U.S. History

Sample Answers
The Treaty of Tordesillas

A Basic Question: What was the effect of this treaty?

1. At that time, Spain and Portugal were the leading seafaring nations of Europe. The most famous explorers of the 15th and 16th centuries—Columbus, Bartholomeu Dias, Vasco da Gama, Amerigo Vespucci, Cortes, Pizarro—came from Spain and Portugal. Portugal's Prince Henry was known as "the Navigator" because of his interest in seagoing explorations. It seemed reasonable to them to assume that they would remain the foremost seagoing nations, and that their explorers would make all major discoveries.

2. Answers will vary. In fact, as might be guessed, rising nations such as England rejected the Spanish and Portuguese claims to all newly discovered territories. In 1497 John Cabot (Giovanni Caboto), a native of Genoa who adopted British nationality, took possession of Newfoundland for England, giving Britain its first claim on the American continent.

3. The Treaty of Tordesillas gave Portugal claim to any landds found in a 1,000-mile-wide swath of ocean. It probably seemed reasonable to assume that such a huge area would offer many new territories for Portuguese colonization, but in fact, most of the new lands fell west of the line of demarcation. The only territory Portugal was able to claim was Brazil, which Pedro Alvares Cabral accidentally discovered in 1500. In the centuries that followed, Brazilian exploration and settlement far to the west of the line set by the Treaty laid the basis for Brazil's claims to vast areas of the interior of South America. By 1500, other nations were beginning to make claims to parts of the continent, ignoring the assertions of Spain and Portugal that any new discoveries should belong to them.

For Further Reading

Morison, Samuel Eliot. *The Great Explorers.* New York: Oxford University Press, 1978.

1620—The Mayflower Compact

In 1620 the English ship the *Mayflower* carried a group of colonists to America. While we often think that all the passengers on the *Mayflower* were committed Puritans, some of the people on board had their own, different reasons for sailing to the new land. There were 101 passengers in all. About 87 of them were Separatists or members of Separatist families. The colonists had been granted territory in Virginia, but storms blew them off course. In November the Pilgrims found themselves off New England, where they had no legal right to land and settle. Nor did they have any plans for governing the colony once they landed. So, while the crew furled the sails, the Pilgrim leaders wrote what we now call the Mayflower Compact. Forty-one men—Pilgrims, hired laborers, and sailors—signed the agreement.

We whose names are underwritten, . . . having undertaken for the glory of God, and advancement of the Christian faith and honor of our king and country, a voyage to plant the first colony in the northern parts of Virginia, do by these presents solemnly and mutually, in the presence of God and one of another, covenant and combine ourselves together into a civil body politic, for our better ordering and preservation and furtherance of the end aforesaid; and by virtue hereof to enact, constitute, and frame such just and equal laws, ordinances, acts, constitutions, offices from time to time as shall be thought most meet and convenient for the general good of the colony; unto which we promise all due submission and obedience. [The Mayflower Compact, 1620]

——Questions——

1. Working singly or in groups, rewrite the Mayflower Compact in your own words. If you want, you can use the glossary or a dictionary to look up unfamiliar words.

2. What different reasons might people have had for sailing to America with the Pilgrims? List as many as you can think of.

3. Why do you think the Pilgrim leaders thought they needed something like the Mayflower Compact?

4. If you had been on board the *Mayflower,* would you have signed the Compact? Why or why not?

5. What significance did the Mayflower Compact have for American government?

GLOSSARY   covenant—agreement
hereof—of this, concerning this
frame—to put together, put into words

ordinances—decrees, directions
furtherance—helping forward, promotion
plant—settle, found a colony

Sample Answers
The Mayflower Compact

A Basic Question: Would you have signed?

1. Answers will vary. By signing the Mayflower Compact, passengers on the *Mayflower* agreed to be ruled by laws considered best for everyone.

2. Most English immigrants came to America for one of three reasons: political reasons, religious reasons, and economic reasons. Those who came for political reasons wanted to find political freedom or to escape the unsettled conditions that resulted from the struggles between kings and Parliament. Those who came for religious reasons wanted to escape religious persecution and to establish communities where they could worship God in their own way. But the most important reasons for emigration to the American colonies were economic. People left England because the enclosure laws pushed many farmers off the lands they had formerly tilled, because inflation made prices too high, and because of widespread unemployment. The emigrants wanted land, jobs, and better lives for themselves and their families.

3. The Pilgrims felt they needed an agreement like this because, even while the *Mayflower* was still at sea, a few passengers had made "mutinous speeches." There were rumors that some of the non-Separatists would defy the Pilgrims if they landed anywhere besides the place specified in the land grant they had received from the London Company. The Compact was a direct response to the threat of divisiveness. Since the colonists knew that they faced considerable difficulty and hardship, they wanted assurance that everyone would be willing to work together for the common good. The Compact was signed by forty-one Pilgrims, hired laborers, and sailors, who agreed to obey whatever laws and officers the community would create. Even so, almost from the first days ashore, there was discontent and murmuring, which the leadership could not finally dispel. Some of the "strangers"—people not primarily committed to religious aims and values—continued to seem different and suspect.

4. Answers will vary. The forty-one signers of the Mayflower Compact included every head of a family, every adult bachelor—including those who had threatened trouble—and most of the hired manservants. The only males who did not sign were those under age, and two sailors who were only obligated to stay for one year. (Females were not invited to sign the Compact.)

5. The Mayflower Compact was the foundation of Plymouth's government, and the first instance of self-government or self-determination in American history. It also contained the germ of the idea of government by consent of the governed, one of the fundamental principles of American government. The significance of the Mayflower Compact lay in the fact that in it, a group of ordinary people took part in making an agreement under which they were to live. For this reason, the document marked an important milestone along the road to government of, by, and for the people. However, the Compact should not be seen as a sort of early Declaration of Independence, with the colonists asserting their rights to self-

government. The Compact stated clearly that the colony was intended for the "advancement of the . . . honor of our king and country."

For Further Reading

Demos, John. *A Little Commonwealth: Family Life in Plymouth Colony.* New York: Oxford University Press, 1970.

UNIT 5

1666—Religious Conformity in the Bay Colony

The Puritans, in America as in England, were proud and demanding. They sought power for Christian purposes. They did not wish to forsake the sinful world and a too-worldly church, they sought to transform them. In 1629, a group of active nonconformists obtained the charter that created the Massachusetts Bay Company, and led to the founding of the Bay Colony. By the middle of the seventeenth century, the Bay Colony was firmly established, with its own system of courts, modeled on the English court system. This excerpt comes from the proceedings of one of these courts in 1666:

Thomas Goold, Thomas Osburne and John George being presented by the grand jury of this county for absenting themselves from the public worship of God on the Lord's days for one whole year now past, alleged respectively as follows.

Thomas Osburne answered, that the reason of his non-attendance was, that the Lord has discovered to him from his word and spirit of truth that the society, wherewith he is now in communion, is more agreeable to the will of God, asserted that they were a church and attended the worship of God together, and do judge themselves bound so to do. . . .

Thomas Goold answered, that as for coming to public worship they did meet in public worship according to the rule of Christ, . . . asserted that they were a public meeting, according to the order of Christ Jesus gathered together.

John George answered, that he did attend the public meetings on the Lord's

days where he was a member; asserted that they were a church according to the order of Christ in the gospel, and with them he walked and held communion in the public worship of God on the Lord's days.

. . . Whereas by their own confessions they stand convicted of persisting in their schismatical assembling themselves together, to the great dishonor of God and our profession of his holy name, contrary to the act of the general court of October last prohibiting them therein on penalty of imprisonment, this court does order their giving bond respectively in £20 each of them, for their appearance to answer their contempt at the next court of assistants.

The above named Thomas Goold, John George, and Thomas Osburne made their appeal to the next court of assistants, and refusing to put in security according to law were committed to prison. [Proceedings of the County Court of Middlesex, April 17, 1666]

——Questions——

1. One reason the Puritans moved to Massachusetts Bay was to be able to worship God as they chose. Based on this excerpt, how do you think the Puritans defined "religious freedom"?

2. What offenses are described in this excerpt? How are they punished?

3. What kind of society do you think developed in the Bay Colony?

GLOSSARY   allege—declare to be true   schismatical—causing division within the church
communion—fellowship

Sample Answers
Religious Conformity in the Bay Colony

A Basic Question: Was this freedom?

1. The Puritans did not believe in "religious freedom," they merely wanted the right to worship as *they* chose. Once they had that right, they tried to impose their own rules of religious worship on all residents of the Colony.

2. The three men were accused of failing to go to church on Sundays for one year, because they attended a group meeting of their own, not the established church. When they persisted in holding their own religious services, bail was set at twenty pounds each. The three men appealed at the next court sitting, and were then imprisoned for failing to pay the bail.

3. The society in the Bay Colony was not a theocracy, as it was never governed directly by the clergy, but church and state, religion and government, were tightly bound. In 1631, the colony's electorate was restricted to church members. In the early years, opposition to the Puritan establishment came from an excess of religious commitment, not a deficiency. In the excerpt given here, Mr. Osburne testified that "the Lord has discovered to him . . . that the society, wherewith he is now in communion, is more agreeable to the will of God." It seems reasonable to assume that Puritan society in the Bay Colony was defined by rigid codes, which could not be transgressed with impunity.

For Further Reading

Elliott, Emory. *Power and the Pulpit in Puritan New England.* Princeton: Princeton University Press, 1975.

Gura, Philip. *A Glimpse of Sion's Glory: Puritan Radicalism in New England, 1620-1660.* Middletown, CT: Wesleyan University Press, 1986.

Pope, Robert. *The Half-Way Covenant: Church Membership in Puritan New England.* Ann Arbor, MI: Books on Demand, 1969.

1692—The Salem Witch Trials

The witch trials of Salem Village, Massachusetts, were America's most notorious episode of witchcraft hysteria. The incident began when some young girls began complaining of sharp pains and accused women in the community of using witchcraft to torment them. A witch-hunting frenzy soon spread. However, since God welcomed the penitent sinner, the Puritan courts were merciful to those who repented. People accused of crime learned that it might be easier to admit guilt and "repent" than to prove their innocence. Within six months of the first hearings, 27 persons had been tried and convicted. Those who refused to confess and repent were executed. One of those condemned was Mary Easty, who sent this petition to her judges.

. . . I petition your honors not for my own life for I know I must die and my appointed time is set but the Lord he knows it is that if it be possible no more innocent blood may be shed which undoubtedly cannot be avoided. In the way and course you go in I question not but your honors do to the utmost of your powers in the discovery and detecting of witchcraft and witches and would not be guilty of innocent blood for the world, but by my own innocence I know you are in the wrong way. The Lord in his infinite mercy direct you in this great work if it be his blessed will that no more innocent blood be shed. I would humbly beg of you that your honors would be pleased to examine these afflicted persons strictly and keep them apart some time and likewise to try some of these confessing witches, I being confident there is several of them has belied themselves and others, as will appear—if not in this world, I am sure in the world to come whither I am now agoing—and I question not but you'll see an alteration of these things. They say myself and others, having made a league with the devil, we cannot confess. I know and the Lord knows as will thoroughly appear they belie me; and so I question not but they do others. The Lord above who is the searcher of all hearts knows that as I shall answer it at the tribunal seat that I know not the least thing of witchcraft therefore I cannot, I dare not belie my own soul. I beg your honors not to deny this my humble petition from a poor dying innocent person and I question not but the Lord will give a blessing to your endeavors. [Petition of Mary Easty, 1692]

——Questions——

1. What reason does Easty give for not saving her life by confessing to witchcraft?

2. What do we mean today by the term "witch hunt"? Can you name any modern witch hunts?

3. What kind of historical, religious, and social factors may have contributed to the development of the Salem witch trials?

GLOSSARY   **belie**—to give a false idea of
endeavor—effort, attempt
league—compact, agreement

petition—request
tribunal—court
whither—towards which

Sample Answers
The Salem Witch Trials

A Basic Question: Why did they happen?

1. She explains that, since she knows nothing of witchcraft, she cannot confess to it. That would be a false confession, which would endanger her soul. She preferred to die rather than perjure herself.

2. We use the term today to signify an investigation, usually conducted with much publicity, supposedly to uncover subversive political activity, disloyalty, etc., but really to harass and weaken the entire political opposition. The Red Scare of 1919 and McCarthyism in the 1950's are two examples of twentieth-century witch hunts.

3. It is important to remember that the witch trials were not, in fact, the aberration they appear from a twentieth-century viewpoint. Medieval Europeans believed very firmly in witchcraft. Between 1480 and 1780, 300,000 witches were executed in Europe. The early immigrants to America brought a belief in witchcraft with them. When the young girls of Salem—who had been told stories of witchcraft by Tituba, a West Indian slave—began to complain of demonic persecution, it was natural for the elders to take them seriously. As the Puritans believed in God, they believed in the Devil as an active, malignant force. The expansion of the accusations in Salem—some 500 people, including the governor's wife, were eventually touched by accusations—might have been caused in part by the Puritan belief in the importance of repentance. Since God welcomed the penitent, so must his representatives here on earth. If an accused woman repented of her sin, she had already averted God's anger; there was no longer much need for the state to punish her. Thus, some of those accused of witchcraft "repented" and "confessed" in order to save their lives. And in order to have something tangible to confess, many implicated other people in their confessions. Mary Easty was originally accused by the afflicted girls. They later changed their minds and denied her complicity, only to accuse her again two days later. The accusations were confirmed by the confessions of other accused witches, and Easty was condemned to death.

For Further Reading

Boyer, Paul, and Stephen Nissembaum. *Salem Possessed: The Social Origins of Witchcraft.* Boston: Harvard University Press, 1974.

Demos, John P. *Entertaining Satan: Witchcraft and the Culture of Early New England.* London: Oxford University Press, 1982.

Hansen, Chadwick. *Witchcraft at Salem.* New York: Braziller, 1985.

Mappen, Marc. *Witches and Historians: Interpretations of Salem Witchcraft.* Melbourne, FL: Krieger, 1980.

Starkey, Marion L. *The Visionary Girls: Witchcraft in Salem Village.* Boston: Little, Brown, 1973.

1735—Peter Zenger

In 1733, John Peter Zenger, a printer, began to publish the *New York Weekly Journal.* The *Journal* soon became openly critical of royal administration in New York. Zenger was charged with libel against the governor. Under existing law, the jury could give a verdict based solely on whether the accused had in fact published the articles; the libel did not have to be false for the accused to be guilty. This excerpt from the *New York Weekly Journal* discusses freedom of the press.

The liberty of the press is a subject of the greatest importance, and in which every individual is as much concerned as he is in any other part of liberty. . . .

There are two sorts of monarchies, an absolute and a limited one. In the first, the liberty of the press can never be maintained, it is inconsistent with it; for what absolute monarch would suffer any subject to animadvert on his actions, when it is in his power to declare the crime, and to nominate the punishment? This would make it very dangerous to exercise such a liberty. . . . Besides, in an absolute monarchy, the will of the prince being the law, a liberty of the press to complain against grievances would be complaining against the law, and the constitution, to which they have submitted, or have been obliged to submit; and therefore, in one sense, may be said to deserve punishment. So that under an absolute monarchy, I say, such a liberty is inconsistent with the constitution, having no proper subject in politics, on which it would be exercised, and if exercised would incur a certain penalty.

But in a limited monarchy, as England is, our laws are known, fixed and established. They are the straight rule and sure guide to direct the king, the ministers, and other his subjects: and therefore an offense against the laws is such an offense against the constitution as ought to receive a proper adequate punishment. [*The New York Weekly Journal,* November 2, 1733]

——Questions——

1. Why do you think public criticism of the governor or legislature might be considered seditious libel?

2. Under the common law of the day, publishing criticism of the governor could be considered seditious libel. Andrew Hamilton acted as Zenger's defense lawyer. What do you think he said in Zenger's defense?

3. Zenger was acquitted. What effect did his acquittal have on American history?

4. What kind of newspaper article would be considered libelous today?

GLOSSARY   **animadvert**—comment critically
   grievance—complaint

nominate—name
seditious—stirring up revolt against authority

Sample Answers
Peter Zenger

A Basic Question: How did the press become free?

1. Publishing criticism of the governor or legislature might make people think ill of their rulers. These disaffected people might then, in the words of the indictment, tend "to raise factions and tumults among the people."

2. Hamilton ignored judicial precedent and based his defense on the fact that the allegations were true. First, he asked permission to prove the truth of the statements in the *Journal.* The court rejected his request, saying "a libel is not to be justified; for it is nevertheless a Libel that is true." Hamilton then declared that the matter at issue was "the Liberty—both of exposing and opposing arbitrary Power (in these Parts of the World, at least) by speaking and writing Truth." He argued that it was not seditious libel for a person to make truthful allegations against the government. The jury overrode the court's instructions and acquitted the prisoner.

3. The Zenger verdict laid the foundation for one of our most cherished traditions—freedom of the press. Hamilton's defense was that true statements did not constitute libel, and that free discussion of public questions was vital to democratic government, two ideas that are very much with us today. Although the Zenger case did not immediately establish freedom of the press, as has been popularly supposed, or put an end to prosecutions for seditious libel, its outcome was of great importance. In the near future liberty of discussion did become an issue, and Zenger's name became a symbol of the individual's right to criticize the government.

4. Answers will vary. An article that, with the intention of damaging an individual's reputation, made untrue allegations about the individual, would probably be construed as libel.

For Further Reading

Alexander, James A. *A Brief Narrative of the Case and Trial of John Peter Zenger, Printer of the New York Weekly,* 2nd edition. Boston: Harvard University Press, 1969.

Buranelli, Vincent, ed. *The Trial of Peter Zenger.* Westport: Greenwood, 1976 (reprint of 1957 edition).

Rutherford, Livingston. *John Peter Zenger: His Press, His Trial, and a Bibliography of Zenger Imprints.* New York: Johnson Reprint, 1970 (reprint of 1904 edition).

UNIT 8
1755—Newcomers and Native Peoples

The first colonists to settle in Massachusetts owed their survival to the help they received from local tribes. Some early colonists even insisted that the colonists had no right to their land unless they bought it from the Indians. But as the number of colonists increased, and they became more knowledgeable about the new land they lived in, relations between Native Americans and Europeans grew worse. This proclamation was made in Boston in 1755.

Given at the Council Chamber in Boston this third day of November 1755 in the twenty-ninth year of the reign of our sovereign lord George the Second. . . .

Whereas the tribe of Penobscot Indians have repeatedly in a perfidious manner acted contrary to their solemn submission unto his Majesty long since made and frequently renewed.

I have, therefore, at the desire of the House of Representatives . . . thought fit to issue this proclamation and to declare the Penobscot Tribe of Indians to be enemies, rebels and traitors to his majesty. . . . And I do hereby require his majesty's subjects of the province to embrace all opportunities of pursuing, captivating, killing and destroying all and every of the aforesaid Indians.

And whereas the General Court of this province have voted that a bounty . . . be granted and allowed to be paid out of the province treasury . . . the premiums of bounty following viz:

For every scalp of a male Indian brought in as evidence for their being killed as aforesaid, forty pounds.

For every scalp of such female Indian or male Indian under the age of twelve years that shall be killed and brought in as evidence of their being killed as aforesaid, twenty pounds. [Proclamation made in Boston, 1755]

——Questions——

1. What do you usually associate with the idea of paying a bounty? What does this tell you about the settlers' opinion of the Penobscots?

2. How do you think the Penobscots viewed the English settlers?

3. The settlers and the Penobscots probably had very different ideas of each group's rights and responsibilities to the other. Can you suggest any way to reconcile these two opinions, and promote peaceful coexistence between the two groups?

4. What other events, occurring at this time, might help explain the repressive attitude towards Native Americans shown in this proclamation?

GLOSSARY
bounty—reward for capturing an outlaw or killing a destructive animal
embrace—take up willingly
perfidious—disloyal, treacherous
proclamation—public announcement
submission—legal agreement
traitor—person who betrays a country or cause
viz—namely

Sample Answers
Newcomers and Native Peoples

A Basic Question: Could their relations have been better?

1. Students will probably associate bounties with trapping certain wild animals that are considered harmful or annoying. Some may think of escaped criminals, or runaway slaves. All of these ideas imply something less than human, or without the rights of a citizen. The idea of paying bounties for scalps is close to the idea of paying for the pelts of wolves, and suggests that the settlers saw the Indians as animals.

2. Many Indian tribes were initially friendly and helpful towards colonists, only to be driven towards resentment. The settlers consistently disregarded agreements made with the Indians when they became inconvenient. Also, individuals felt no compunction about tricking or defrauding Indians. By the time this proclamation was made, the Indians probably felt that the settlers were trying to deprive them of their lands.

3. Answers will vary. Students may suggest that, if the settlers began to treat the Indians as human beings, and to honor their commitments to them, the situation would probably improve.

4. The Seven Years' War, also known as the French and Indian War, began in July 1755, when a combined force of French and Indians ambushed General Edward Braddock and his troops in the Ohio country, near what is now Pittsburgh. The harshness of this document may stem in part from colonists' reaction to an alliance between the Indians and the French, hereditary enemies of the British. However, it must also be remembered that bounties for Indian scalps in Massachusetts went back at least as far as 1703, when a scalp brought twelve pounds sterling.

For Further Reading

Axtell, James. *The Invasion Within: The Contest of Cultures in Colonial America.* New York: Oxford University Press, 1985.

Glasrud, Bruce, and Alan Smith. *Race Relations in British North America, 1607-1783.* Chicago: Nelson-Hall, 1982.

Nash, Gary. *Red, White and Black: The Peopling of Early America.* New York: Prentice-Hall, 1974.

Peckham, Howard, and Charles Gibson, eds. *Attitudes of Colonial Powers Toward the American Indian.* Salt Lake City: University of Utah Press, 1976.

1765—The Stamp Act

The reorganization of the British Empire begun in 1763 called for raising additional money in the American colonies. The Stamp Act was designed to raise an additional £60,000.

... Be it enacted ..., that from and after [November 1, 1765] there shall be raised, levied, collected, and paid unto his Majesty, his heirs, and successors, throughout the colonies and plantations in America which now are, or hereafter may be, under the dominion of his Majesty, his heirs and successors,

For every skin or piece of vellum or parchment, or sheet or piece of paper, on which shall be ingrossed, written or printed, any declaration, plea, replication, rejoinder, demurrer, or other pleading, or any copy thereof, in any court of law within the British colonies and plantations in America, a stamp duty of three pence. . . .

For every advertisement to be contained in any gazette, newspaper, or other paper, or any pamphlet . . . , a duty of two shillings.

And be it further enacted . . . That no matter or thing whatsoever, by this act charged with the payment of a duty, shall be pleaded or given in evidence, or admitted in any court within the said colonies and plantations, to be good, useful, or available in law or equity, unless the same shall be marked or stamped, in pursuance of this act, with the respective duty hereby charged thereon, or with an higher duty. . . . [The Stamp Act, March 22, 1765]

——Questions——

1. Based on the excerpt quoted here, what do you think was the general purpose of the Stamp Act?

2. The Stamp Act wasn't the first Act of Parliament that the colonists found oppressive. The Molasses Act of Parliament placed high duties on sugar and molasses imported from the non-British West Indies. The Woolens Act of 1699 forbade the shipment of woolen goods, even to neighboring colonies. The Hat Act of 1732 prohibited the sale of hats and felts outside of the colony in which they were made. The colonists resented these restrictions. Why do you think the British might have imposed them?

3. Although the earlier acts were resented, they did not arouse such an active response as the Stamp Act. Why did the Stamp Act cause such discord?

4. Section LVII of the Stamp Act specified that offenses against any acts relating to trade could be prosecuted in the admiralty courts. These courts were presided over by a single judge, and did not require a jury. Why do you think this clause might have been resented by the Americans?

5. If you had been alive in 1765, would you have opposed the Stamp Act? If so, how would you have expressed your opposition?

GLOSSARY **demurrer**—legal statement
dominion—domain, territory
gazette—newspaper
levy—impose, collect
parchment—writing material made of skin
plantation—colony, settlement

pleading—legal statement
pursuance—carrying out, putting into effect
rejoinder—legal statement; answer
replication—legal statement; reply
thereon—on it
vellum—writing material made of skin

Sample Answers
The Stamp Act

A Basic Question: Was it just?

1. To require the colonists to pay for a stamp on all documents.

2. From Britain's point of view, these acts were perfectly appropriate. Parliament was not trying to punish the colonies by regulating their economic life. English statesmen, naturally, believed that the mother country was more important than its colonies. Britain did not consider the American colonies any more important than her empire in India, or her possessions in the West Indies. The British felt that colonial trade with other countries—especially colonial purchases elsewhere of goods that were also made in England—resulted in economic loss.

3. The Stamp Act differed from earlier acts of Parliament in that it was the first attempt to raise revenue within the colonies by direct taxation. The British believed that Parliament had the right to pass legislation for all parts of the Empire. The colonists drew a distinction between legislation and taxation. They argued that Parliament could legislate for them but could not tax them, since it did not represent them. The British believed in the theory of virtual representation, that is, each member of Parliament represented all Englishmen no matter where they lived. The Americans believed in the theory of actual representation. They claimed that they were not represented in the British government because there was no member of Parliament selected from the thirteen colonies to present their views there. The colonists insisted that the colonies were bound to England by personal union with the Crown, rather than by legislative union through Parliament. These differences explain why the colonists argued that there could be no taxation except through their own colonial legislatures.

   The Stamp Act also offended on several other grounds. First, it was obvious that England would strictly enforce this Act. Earlier restrictive acts had been treated with lenience, and infringements had been ignored. But George III had ascended the throne in 1760, and was determined to increase his royal authority by stricter supervision of the colonies.

4. Under English law, the right to a jury trial goes back to 1215 and the Magna Carta. The Stamp Act withdrew that right. Americans saw this as unjust for two reasons. First, it was said that admiralty judges took commission on all condemnations. Thus, they would gain financially by convicting. And second, the act was seen as making distinctions between the rights of English subjects living in America and those who lived in Britain. Americans resented this implication that they were "second-class citizens."

5. Answers will vary. Patrick Henry was one of the first to respond to the Stamp Act, with his Virginia Stamp Act Resolves. The Virginia House of Burgesses passed four of Henry's seven proposals in late May, declaring that the colonists had never forfeited the rights of British citizens, and consent to taxation was one of those rights. The reaction of other people went farther. In August, demonstrators in Boston tore down the building they thought was intended as the stamp office, broke the windows of the province's stamp distributor—prompting him to refuse to carry out the duties of his office—and completely destroyed the townhouse of Lieutenant Governor Thomas Hutchinson. Demonstrations against the Stamp Act occurred in cities and towns stretching from Halifax, Nova Scotia, to the

Caribbean island of Antigua. They were so successful that, by November 1, when the law was scheduled to take effect, not a single stamp distributor was willing to carry out the duties of the office. Thus the act could not be enforced.

Resistance also took other forms. Colonial legislatures petitioned Parliament to repeal the Stamp Act. The Sons of Liberty, an intercolonial association, was formed to channel resistance into acceptable forms. They held mass meetings to win public support for the resistance movement. And American merchants organized nonimportation associations to put economic pressure on British exporters. Many individuals refused to use items imported from Britain.

For Further Reading

Langguth, A. J. *Patriots: The Men Who Started the American Revolution.* New York: Simon and Schuster, 1988.

Maier, Pauline M. *From Resistance to Revolution: Colonial Radicals and the Development of American Opposition to Britain, 1765-1776.* New York: Random House, 1973.

Morgan, Edmund S. and Helen M. *The Stamp Act Crisis: Prologue to Revolution.* New York: Macmillan, 1983.

1770—The Boston Massacre

In October 1768, royal troops began arriving in Massachusetts. The soldiers were in Boston to keep order, but townspeople saw them as potential oppressors. Brawls became common. On the evening of March 5, 1770, a group of men and boys started throwing rocks and snowballs at a single sentry in front of the customs house.

. . . there was much foul language between them, and some of them, in consequence of his pushing at them with his bayonet, threw snowballs at him, which occasioned him to knock hastily at the door of the Custom House. From hence two persons thereupon proceeded immediately to the main-guard, which was posted opposite to the State House, at a small distance, near the head of the said street.

The officer on guard was Capt. Preston, who with seven or eight soldiers, with fire-arms and charged bayonets, issued from the guard-house, and in great haste posted himself and his soldiers in front of the Custom House, near the corner aforesaid. In passing to this station the soldiers pushed several persons with their bayonets, driving through the people in so rough a manner that it appeared they intended to create a disturbance. This occasioned some snowballs to be thrown at them, which seems to have been the only provocation that was given. . . .

The said party was formed into a half circle; and within a short time after they had been posted at the Custom House, began to fire upon the people.

Captain Preston is said to have ordered them to fire, and to have repeated that order. One gun was fired first; then others in succession, and with deliberation, till ten or a dozen guns were fired; or till that number of discharges were made from the guns that were fired. By which means eleven persons were killed and wounded, as above represented. [*A Short Narrative of the Horrid Massacre in Boston*, 1770]

—Questions—

1. This account pretends to give a fair account of the incident. At what points do the writers seem to make a show of objectivity? What influence do you think that apparent objectivity would have on the reader?

2. John Adams defended the soldiers; all but two of them were acquitted. His willingness to defend them is often held up as an example of his great moral strength. Why do you think defending these men might have called for moral courage?

3. The soldiers were tried in an American court, defended by an American lawyer, and acquitted. Yet the Boston Massacre roused many Americans to anger against Britain. Why do you think that might be?

4. Although the word "massacre" usually means "killing a great number," only five people died as a result of this incident. How do you think it came to be called "The Boston Massacre"? Do you think public reaction might have been different if it had been called "The Boston Incident"?

GLOSSARY   **bayonet**—a knife attached to the muzzle end of a rifle
deliberation—care and slowness
discharge—firing a weapon

occasion—cause, bring about
provocation—cause of anger or aggression
succession—one after the other
thereupon—after that

Sample Answers
The Boston Massacre

A Basic Question: Was it a massacre?

1. The authors say, in reference to the snowballs, "which seems to have been the only provocation that was given." This does not say, categorically, that there was no other provocation. By seeming to leave the matter slightly open, the authors imply that they only want to state what they know to be true. There may have been some other provocation which the authors have not heard of, they will not rule out the possibility, but none of the scores of individuals to whom they spoke had seen any. The same effect is produced in the last paragraph of the excerpt, where the authors say "till ten or a dozen guns were fired; or till that number of discharges were made from the guns that were fired." Again, they seem unwilling to commit themselves to an absolute statement which they cannot verify.

2. The soldiers, and their actions, were vilified. Since the general impression was that they were guilty, Adams was risking a great deal by agreeing to defend them. As a lawyer, he depended on the people of Boston for his clients. He risked alienating current and future clients by accepting the soldiers' defense. He also jeopardized his political career, as critics suggested that he had sold out his principles for a fat legal fee. In fact, Adams received only eighteen guineas for his services, but he did not defend himself by revealing this fact.

3. The "Boston Massacre" was promptly made the subject of anti-British propaganda, including the account excerpted here, and Paul Revere's well-known engraving of the massacre. These accounts were not very believable, but aimed to arouse an emotional response. For many colonists, the engraving provided their only knowledge of the incident. With newspapers scarce, and many colonists illiterate, a graphic image like this gave many people an erroneous impression of events.

4. Answers will vary. The use of the word "massacre" was probably a deliberate element of the anti-British propaganda, designed to rouse people's emotions even more against the British soldiers.

For Further Reading

A Short Narrative of the Horrid Massacre in Boston. Williamstown, MA: Corner House, 1973 (reprint of 1849 edition).

Zobel, Hiller B. *The Boston Massacre.* New York: Norton, 1970.

1774—Logan's Speech

Captain John Logan, or Tahgagjute, was a leader of the Mingo, bands of Iroquois-speaking Indians who lived in western Pennsylvania. Logan became a vigorous defender of the whites. But when his kinspeople were slaughtered by colonists during the Yellow Creek Massacre of 1774, Logan became embittered. He made retaliatory raids against American settlers. After he was defeated at the Battle of Point Pleasant, Pennsylvania, he delivered this message to Lord Dunmore's winning forces.

I appeal to any white man to say, if ever he entered Logan's cabin hungry, and he gave him not meat: if ever he came cold and naked, and he clothed him not. During the course of the last long and bloody war Logan remained idle in his cabin, an advocate for peace. Such was my love for the whites, that my countrymen pointed as they passed, and said, "Logan is the friend of white men." I had even thought to have lived with you, but for the injuries of one man. Colonel Cresap, the last spring, in cold blood, and unprovoked, murdered all the relations of Logan, not even sparing my women and children. There runs not a drop of my blood in the veins of any living creature. This called on me for revenge. I have sought it: I have killed many: I have fully glutted my vengeance: for my country I rejoice at the beams of peace. But do not harbor a thought that mine is the joy of fear. Logan never felt fear. He will not turn on his heel to save his life. Who is there to mourn for Logan? Not one. [Speech by Captain John Logan, October 1774]

——Questions——

1. Logan's speech describes, in one man's experience, the pattern of Native American-European relationships. What five steps in this pattern can you see in the speech and subsequent events as described in the introduction?

2. Logan did not personally deliver his message to Lord Dunmore. It was translated and presented by General John Gibson, the Virginia emissary sent to arrange for peace. Critics have charged that "your Logan speech, your fine specimen of Indian oratory, is a lie, a counterfeit, and never in fact had any existence as a real Indian speech!" The speech was delivered, and subsequently published, in translation, not in the language in which Logan actually spoke. Do you think this affects the validity of the speech itself?

GLOSSARY   **advocate**—supporter
         glut—fill beyond capacity

unprovoked—without incitement
vengeance—revenge

Sample Answers
Logan's Speech

A Basic Question: Was it genuine?

1. a) Befriending of whites by Native Americans
    b) Attack on Native Americans by individuals or groups seeking to expand European holdings
    c) Violent revenge taken by Native Americans
    d) Punitive military expedition to quell the "Indian uprising"
    e) Defeat of Native Americans, followed by loss of land

2. Answers will vary.

For Further Reading

Sosin, Jack M. *Whitehall and the Wilderness: The Middle West in British Colonial Policy, 1760-1775.* Westport: Greenwood, 1981 (reprint of 1961 edition).

Vanderwerth, W.C. *Indian Oratory: A Collection of Famous Speeches by Noted Indian Chieftains.* Norman, OK: University of Oklahoma Press, 1972.

1775—The Battle of Lexington

These extracts present the official American and English versions, respectively, of the hostilities at Lexington, April 19, 1775.

Friends and fellow subjects—Hostilities are at length commenced in this colony by the troops under the command of general Gage. . . .

By the clearest depositions relative to this transaction, it will appear that on the night preceding the nineteenth of April instant, a body of the king's troops, under the command of colonel Smith, were secretly landed at Cambridge, with an apparent design to take or destroy the military and other stores, provided for the defence of this colony, and deposited at Concord—that some inhabitants of the colony, on the night aforesaid, whilst travelling peaceably on the road, between Boston and Concord, were seized and greatly abused by armed men, who appeared to be officers of general Gage's army; that the town of Lexington, by these means, was alarmed, and a company of the inhabitants mustered on the occasion—that the regular troops on their way to Concord, marched into the said town of Lexington, and the said company, on this approach, began to disperse—that, notwithstanding this, the regulars rushed on with great violence and first began hostilities, by firing on said Lexington company, whereby they killed eight, and wounded several others—that the regulars continued their fire, until those of said company, who were neither killed nor wounded, had made their escape—that colonel Smith, with the detachment then marched to Concord, where a number of provincials were again fired on by the troops, produced an engagement that lasted through the day, in which many of the provincials and more of the regular troops were killed and wounded.

To give a particular account of the ravages of the troops, as they retreated from Concord to Charlestown, would be very difficult, if not impracticable; let it suffice to say, that a great number of the houses on the road were plundered and rendered unfit for use, several were burnt, women in child-bed were driven by the soldiery naked into the streets, old men peaceably in their houses were shot dead, and such scenes exhibited as would disgrace the annals of the most uncivilized nation. [Account by the Provincial Congress at Watertown, Massachusetts, April 26, 1775]

Sir,—In obedience to your Excellency's command, I marched on the evening of the 18th inst. with the corps of grenadiers and light infantry for Concord, to execute your Excellency's orders with respect to destroying all ammunition, artillery, tents, &c, collected there. . . .

. . . When I had got some miles on the march from Boston, I detached six light infantry companies to march with all expedition to seize the two bridges on different roads beyond Concord. On these companies' arrival at Lexington . . . they found on a green close to the road a body of the country people drawn up in military order, with arms and accoutrements, and, as appeared after, loaded; and that they had posted some men in a dwelling and Meeting-house. Our troops advanced towards them, without any intention of injuring them, further than to inquire the reason of their being thus assembled, and, if not satisfactory, to have secured their arms; but they in confusion went off, principally to the left, only one of them fired before he went off, and three or four men jumped over a wall and fired from behind it among the soldiers; on which the troops returned it, and killed several of them. They

(continued)

1775—The Battle of Lexington
(continued)

likewise fired on the soldiers from the Meeting and dwelling-houses. . . . While at Concord we saw vast numbers assembling in many parts; at one of the bridges they marched down, with a very considerable body, on the light infantry posted there. On their coming pretty near, one of our men fired on them, which they returned; on which an action ensued, and some few were killed and wounded. In this affair, it appears that, after the bridge was quitted, they scalped and otherwise ill-treated one or two of the men who were either killed or severely wounded. . . . On our leaving Concord to return to Boston, they began to fire on us from behind the walls, ditches, trees, &c, which, as we marched, increased to a very great degree, and continued without intermission of five minutes altogether, for, I believe, upwards of eighteen miles. . . . Notwithstanding the enemy's numbers, they did not make one gallant attempt during so long an action, though our men were so very much fatigued, but kept under cover. [Report of Lieutenant-Colonel Smith to Governor Gage, April 22, 1775]

——Questions——

1. Both these excerpts describe the same event, but they give very different versions. Why do you think they are so different?

2. What might have been the intention of the people who wrote these accounts?

3. Do you think the writers of these excerpts were trying to give unbiased accounts of the events of April 19? Refer to specific passages to support your opinion.

4. Compare the two accounts, and try to decide what actually happened. Then write your own account of the Battles of Lexington and Concord.

GLOSSARY

accouterments—equipment
deposition—testimony
detachment—body of troops
disperse—separate, move off
engagement—battle
gallant—brave
grenadier—soldier carrying grenades
hostilities—open warfare
impracticable—not able to be done

infantry—soldiers trained to fight on foot
muster—gather
instant—the current month
notwithstanding—in spite of
plunder—rob
provincial—country person
ravage—severe damage
regulars—soldiers
transaction—operation

Sample Answers
The Battle of Lexington

A Basic Question: What actually happened?

1. They are different because they were written by people on opposing sides in the struggle.

2. They were trying to present their own side in the best possible light.

3. Answers will vary. Students will probably agree that the authors were not trying to give unbiased accounts. In the first excerpt, the paragraph beginning "To give a particular account . . ." is obviously designed to appeal to the emotions of the reader, and to present the British soldiers as brutes. In the second excerpt the sentence beginning "Our troops advanced towards them, without any intention of injuring them . . ." is unbelievably disingenuous. The British officers could not really believe that the advance of armed soldiers on a defense force would not be seen as offensive.

4. Answers will vary. A possible response might be: Lieutenant-Colonel Francis Smith led a British column from Boston to seize the gunpowder of the Massachusetts Provincial Congress at Concord. On the morning of April 19, Smith's redcoats scattered a company of local Minutemen at Lexington, killing several when unauthorized firing occurred; it is not known which side fired first. At Concord, Smith managed to find only part of the gunpowder because news of his mission had been carried to the countryside by Paul Revere and his associates. As they returned to Boston, the British were under constant assault from Massachusetts militiamen, who inflicted 273 casualties.

For Further Reading

Countryman, Edward. *The American Revolution*. New York: Hill & Wang, 1985.

Morgan, Edmund S. *The Challenge of the American Revolution*. New York: Norton, 1976.

1776—Thomas Paine's *Common Sense*

Thomas Paine's pamphlet *Common Sense* summed up the feelings of many Americans about Britain. In it, Paine urged open revolt against the "Royal Brute of England." Within months, 100,000 copies of *Common Sense* had been sold in the colonies, which had a population of two and a half million—many of them illiterate.

As much hath been said of the advantages of reconciliation, which, like an agreeable dream, hath passed away and left us as we were, it is but right, that we should examine the contrary side of the argument, and inquire into some of the many material injuries which these colonies sustain, and always will sustain, by being connected with, and dependant on Great-Britain: To examine that connexion and dependance, on the principles of nature and common sense, to see what we have to trust to, if separated, and what we are to expect, if dependant.

I have heard it asserted by some, that as America hath flourished under her former connexion with Great-Britain, that the same connexion is necessary towards her future happiness, and will always have the same effect. Nothing can be more fallacious than this kind of argument. We may as well assert that because a child has thrived upon milk, that it is never to have meat, or that the first twenty years of our lives is to become a precedent for the next twenty. But even this is admitting more than is true, for I answer roundly, that America would have flourished as much, and probably much more, had no European power had any thing to do with her. The commerce, by which she hath enriched herself, are the necessaries of life, and will always have a market while eating is the custom of Europe.

. . . As to government matters, it is not in the power of Britain to do this continent justice: The business of it will soon be too weighty, and intricate, to be managed with any tolerable degree of convenience, by a power so distant from us, and so very ignorant of us; for if they cannot conquer us, they cannot govern us. To be always running three or four thousand miles with a tale or a petition, waiting four or five months for an answer, which when obtained requires five or six more to explain it in, will in a few years be looked upon as folly and childishness—There was a time when it was proper, and there is a proper time for it to cease.

Small islands not capable of protecting themselves, are the proper objects for kingdoms to take under their care, but there is something very absurd, in supposing a continent to be perpetually governed by an island. In no instance hath nature made the satellite larger than its primary planet, and as England and America, with respect to each other, reverses the common order of nature, it is evident they belong to different systems; England to Europe, America to itself. [*Common Sense*, 1776]

——Questions——

1. Why do you think Paine called his pamphlet "Common Sense"? How do you think the title might have affected the force of his arguments?

2. What arguments does Paine present in this excerpt from the pamphlet?

3. This excerpt contains two powerful analogies. What are they? How do they work to strengthen Paine's arguments?

(continued)

1776—Thomas Paine's *Common Sense*
(continued)

——Questions——

4. Although the language may seem difficult, the arguments presented here are very clear. Rewrite the excerpt in your own words, keeping the sense of the original.

GLOSSARY

brute—cruel person
commerce—business
connexion—connection
contrary—different, opposite
fallacious—illogical
flourish—grow well
hath—has
intricate—complex

material—important
petition—request
precedent—model
reconciliation—coming back into agreement
satellite—small planet revolving around a larger one
thrive—grow well
tolerable—adequate

Sample Answers
Thomas Paine's *Common Sense*

A Basic Question: Did it make sense?

1. In *Common Sense*, Paine used striking comparisons in a matter-of-fact way to make his arguments. He could have used a title like "Some Detailed Political Arguments in Favor of Dissolution of the Control of the Monarchy in This Continent," but this would have reduced the force of his arguments. By saying, in effect, "This is nothing special, it's nothing you wouldn't have thought of yourself," Paine made his readers more open to accepting his arguments.

2. a) Just because we have done well so far while connected with Great Britain, we can't assume that we will continue to do so.
   b) Since American goods are essential to Europe, we probably would have done better without England all along.
   c) The distance between us is too great to allow Britain to direct American affairs.
   d) It is ridiculous to think that a country as large as America should be ruled by a small island like Britain.
   e) England is part of Europe, America is not, and the two countries should no longer be connected.

3. In the second paragraph, Paine compares America to a child. All children are fed at first on milk, but that is only until they are strong; then they are given solid foods. In the same way, it made a certain degree of sense not to give America autonomy when the colonies were small and weak, but this is no longer the case. The colonies are now mature enough to direct their own affairs. This is a homey argument that any reader could understand; it requires no knowledge of politics or economics. The simplicity of the analogy gives it strength.

   In the final paragraph, England and America are compared to a planet and its satellite. As nature has never made a planet which is dwarfed by its own satellite, so it is not natural that England should continue to rule America. This analogy conveys a strong visual image, of a tiny planet with a huge satellite circling around it. This is so obviously ridiculous, it adds force to Paine's argument that England should not govern America.

4. Answers will vary. A possible response might be:

   A lot has been said about reconciling with Britain, but the very idea of reconciliation is no longer a reality. Still, it would be only fair to look at the other side of the argument: how are the colonies injured by being connected with Great Britain? What could we expect, if we separated from Britain?

   I have heard some people say that, since America has grown and flourished under British direction, British control will always be good for America. You might as well say that because a baby thrives on milk, it should be kept on milk as an adult, and never given meat. And besides, I think that America would probably have fared even better without British direction. The commodities we produce are so basic, they will always find a market in Europe.

   As to government, Britain is too far away and too ignorant of our affairs to be able to handle them. It doesn't make sense to have to go three or four thousand miles about every little thing, wait four or five months for an answer, and another five or six months for an explanation of the answer. There was a time when this was appropriate, but it should stop now.

It makes sense for a kingdom to manage the affairs of small islands which can't protect themselves, but it is ridiculous to think of an island ruling a continent. It would be like having an enormous satellite orbiting a tiny planet, and would be against nature. It is obvious that America and England are not parts of the same whole, but completely separate things. England is part of Europe, and America stands by itself.

For Further Reading

Foner, Eric. *Tom Paine and the American Revolution.* New York: Oxford University Press, 1976.

Paine, Thomas. *Common Sense, The Rights of Man and Other Essential Writings.* New York: Meridian, 1984.

1776—The Declaration of Independence

Here is an excerpt from Thomas Jefferson's first draft of the Declaration of Independence. This material was not included in the version adopted by Congress.

He has waged cruel war against human nature itself, violating it's most sacred rights of life & liberty in the persons of a distant people who never offended him, captivating & carrying them into slavery in another hemisphere, or to incur miserable death in their transportation thither. This piratical warfare, the opprobrium of *infidel* powers, is the warfare of the CHRISTIAN king of Great Britain. Determined to keep open a market where MEN should be bought and sold, he has prostituted his negative for suppressing every legislative attempt to prohibit or to restrain this execrable commerce: and that this assemblage of horrors might want no fact of distinguished die, he is now exciting those very people to rise in arms among us, and to purchase that liberty of which *he* has deprived them, by murdering the people upon whom *he* also obtruded them; thus paying off former crimes committed against the *liberties* of one people, with crimes which he urges them to commit against the *lives* of another. [Draft of the Declaration of Independence, 1776]

——Questions——

1. What is Jefferson talking about in this passage?

2. Why do you think this section was not included in the final draft?

3. How do you think American history might have been different if the Declaration had been adopted as Jefferson originally wrote it?

4. Look at a copy of the Declaration of Independence as it was accepted by Congress. What do you think was the overall purpose of the Declaration of Independence?

5. State four principles of the Declaration of Independence. Give an example of a recent event in the United States that shows one of those principles in use today.

GLOSSARY   **assemblage**—collection
    captivate—capture
    excite—arouse, incite
    execrable—terrible, hateful
    hemisphere—half of the earth
    infidel—not Christian
    obtrude—force upon
    opprobrium—shame, disgrace

prostituted his negative—misused his veto power
suppress—hold back, check
thither—there
to want no fact of distinguished die—to lack no impressive facts
violate—break, disregard
wage—carry on

        Cases and Controversies in U.S. History

Sample Answers
The Declaration of Independence

A Basic Question: Was the best draft used?

1. He is talking about slavery.

2. Many of the most influential people of the time, including Jefferson himself, were slaveholders. It was essential that Congress accept the Declaration, and the committee feared that the denunciation of slavery might alienate some members. At the time, Jefferson wrote that this passage "was struck out in complaisance to South Carolina and Georgia, who had never attempted to restrain the importation of slaves, and who on the contrary still wished to continue it. Our Northern brethren also I believe felt a little tender under those censures, for tho' their people have very few slaves themselves yet they have been pretty considerable carriers of them to others."

3. Answers will vary. Students may suggest that there would have been no Civil War, and that the economic and agricultural development of the southern states would have been very different. Some may feel that the Declaration of Independence would not have been accepted as it stood, or that two separate countries, one slaveholding and one free, would have developed out of the War of Independence.

4. The Declaration of Independence was designed as a powerful piece of propaganda. It was an attempt to win public support, in both America and Europe, for American independence. For this reason England and the English king were painted as evil and aggressive, while the colonies were patient and long-suffering. It also contained the outline of a new theory of government, and a declaration of war against Britain. Writing about the Declaration later, Jefferson said that the intention was not to say something new, but "to place before mankind the common sense of the subject, in terms so plain and firm as to command their assent . . . . Neither aiming at originality of principles or sentiments, nor yet copied from any particular and previous writing, it was intended to be an expression of the American mind."

5. Answers will vary.

For Further Reading

Malone, Dumas. *Jefferson and His Time: The Sage of Monticello.* 6 vols. Boston: Little, Brown, 1948-1981.

Peterson, Marshall D., ed. *The Portable Thomas Jefferson.* New York: Viking, 1975.

Wills, Garry. *Inventing America: Jefferson's Declaration of Independence.* Garden City, NY: Doubleday, 1978.

1776—Women's Rights and the Revolution

When John Adams was serving in the Continental Congress, he corresponded regularly with his wife, Abigail:

Abigail to John

I long to hear that you have declared independency—and, by the way, in the new code of laws, which I suppose it will be necessary for you to make, I desire you would Remember the Ladies, be more generous and favorable to them than your ancestors. Do not put such unlimited power into the hands of Husbands. Remember all men would be Tyrants if they could. If particular care is not paid to Ladies, we are determined to foment a Revolution, and we will not hold ourselves bound by any laws in which we have no voice or representation.

That your sex are naturally tyrannical is a truth so thoroughly established as to admit of no dispute. But such of you as wish to be happy willingly give up the harsh title of master for the more tender and endearing one of friend. Why, then, not put it out of the power of the vicious and the lawless to use us with cruelty and indignity . . . ? Men of sense in all ages abhor those customs which treat us only as the vassals of your sex. Regard us then as beings, placed by providence under your protection, and in imitation of the Supreme Being make use of that power only for our happiness. [Letter from Abigail Adams to John Adams, March 31, 1776]

John to Abigail

. . . As to your extraordinary code of laws, I cannot but laugh. We have been told that our struggle has loosened the bands of government everywhere. . . . Depend upon it, we know better than to repeal our masculine systems. Although they are in full force, you know they are little more than theory. We dare not exert our power in its full latitude. We are obliged to go fair and softly, and in practice, you know, we are the subjects.

We have only the name of masters, and rather than give up this, which would completely subject us to the despotism of the petticoat, I hope General Washington, and all our brave heroes would fight. I am sure every good politician would plot, as long as he would against despotism, empire, monarchy, aristocracy, oligarchy, or ochlocracy—a fine story indeed. [Letter from John Adams to Abigail Adams, April 14, 1776]

——Questions——

1. What does this exchange of letters tell you about the status of women in revolutionary America?

2. What kind of laws do you think Abigail Adams might have wanted to see enacted?

3. John Adams was a member of the committee that wrote the Declaration of Independence, which begins with the words, "We hold these truths to be self-evident: that all men are created equal . . ." Do you think that the committee members meant to limit equality to men, or that they meant all men and all women?

(continued)

1776—Women's Rights and the Revolution
(continued)

4. Write a letter from Abigail to John in response to his letter quoted here. In it, give the best arguments you can think of for considering the rights of women in the laws of the new nation.

5. How do you think Abigail Adams would react if she knew about the position of women in America today? Name three ways in which you think the position of women has changed, for better or worse, since colonial days, and three ways in which you think the position of women has stayed the same.

GLOSSARY

ancestor—person from whom one is descended
despotism—government by absolute power
endearing—making dear
foment—stir up
indignity—wound to pride

latitude—scope
ochlocracy—mob rule
oligarchy—rule by a small group of people
providence—divine direction
tyrant—cruel ruler
vassal—person who is subject to another

Sample Answers
Women's Rights and the Revolution

A Basic Question: Were women treated fairly?

1. From this exchange of letters, the reader can deduce that women in revolutionary America had very little personal freedom. Abigail describes women as the "vassals" of men, who are known by the title of "master." She asks that John, and the others responsible for the laws of the new nation, should not "put such unlimited power into the hands of husbands." This would seem to imply that, once a woman married, her husband had complete control over her affairs. When the husband was a just and considerate man, the woman might not be harmed by such an arrangement; but when the husband, as no doubt often happened, was more interested in control than consideration, he could treat the wife very poorly indeed. Lawmakers probably argued that women could not handle their own affairs, but there are many instances in early America of widows capably carrying on the affairs of their husbands—including Ann Franklin, widow of Ben's brother, who kept her husband's printshop going after his death.

2. Answers will vary. Students may answer that Abigail would have liked women to be allowed control over their affairs, the right to vote, etc., in keeping with the ideas of equality put forth in the Declaration of Independence.

3. Answers will vary. Students may answer that the wording of the Declaration of Independence was chosen very carefully. A spirited denunciation of slavery, implying that "all men" included "black men," was removed from the original draft. If women were not specifically mentioned in the Declaration, they were probably not meant to be included.

4. Answers will vary.

5. Answers will vary.

For Further Reading

Butterfield, L.H. et al., eds. *The Book of Abigail and John: Selected Letters of the Adams Family, 1762-1784.* Boston: Harvard University Press, 1975.

DePauw, Linda Grant. *Founding Mothers: Women of America in the Revolutionary Era.* Boston: Houghton Mifflin, 1975.

Kerber, Linda K. *Women of the Republic: Intellect and Ideology in Revolutionary America.* Chapel Hill: University of North Carolina Press, 1980.

Levin, Phyllis Lee. *Abigail Adams: A Biography.* New York: St. Martin's, 1987.

Norton, Mary Beth. *Liberty's Daughters: The Revolutionary Experience of American Women, 1750-1800.* Boston: Little, Brown, 1980.

1796—Washington's Farewell Address

The Farewell Address is considered one of America's most important historic documents. It set a sensible course for the young and still weak country, and shaped American foreign policy in many ways.

. . . Observe good faith and justice toward all nations. Cultivate peace and harmony with all. . . . It will be worthy of a free, enlightened, and at no distant period a great nation to give to mankind the magnanimous and too novel example of a people always guided by an exalted justice and benevolence. . . .

In the execution of such a plan nothing is more essential than that permanent, inveterate antipathies against particular nations and passionate attachments for others should be excluded, and that in place of them just and amicable feelings toward all should be cultivated. . . . Antipathy in one nation against another disposes each one readily to offer insult and umbrage, and to be haughty and intractable when accidental or trifling occasions of dispute occur. . . .

So, likewise, a passionate attachment of one nation for another produces a variety of evils. Sympathy for the favorite nation, facilitating the illusion of an imaginary common interest where no real common interest exists, and infusing into one the enmities of the other, betrays the former into a participation in the quarrels and wars of the latter without adequate inducement or justification. . . . The great rule of conduct for us in regard to foreign nations is, in extending our commercial relations to have with them as little political connection as possible. So far as we have already formed engagements let them be fulfilled with perfect good faith. Here let us stop. . . .

Our detached and distant situation invites and enables us to pursue a different course. . . . Why forego the advantages of so peculiar a situation? Why quit our own to stand upon foreign ground? Why, by interweaving our destiny with that of any part of Europe, entangle our peace and prosperity in the toils of European ambition, rivalship, interest, humor, or caprice? [George Washington's Farewell Address, September 17, 1796]

——Questions——

1. In your own words, what are the three main points Washington makes in this excerpt?

2. What influence do you think this speech might have had on American foreign policy?

3. When and why did the U.S. abandon Washington's advice as to European politics and permanent alliances?

4. To what extent is Washington's advice still valid today?

GLOSSARY

amicable—friendly
antipathy—dislike, opposition
benevolence—kindliness
caprice—impulsive change of mind
cultivate—develop
enlightened—freed from ignorance
enmity—hatred, hostility
entangle—involve in something complicated, snarl
exalted—lofty, noble
execution—carrying out
facilitate—make easier
forego—give up, do without

harmony—good will, accord
haughty—proud and vain, arrogant
illusion—mistaken notion
inducement—incentive, motive
interweave—weave or twine together
intractable—stubborn
inveterate—firmly established
justification—good reason
magnanimous—unselfish and gracious
novel—unusual
rivalship—competition
trifling—slight
umbrage—offense

Sample Answers
Washington's Farewell Address

A Basic Question: Was he correct?

1. The three main points Washington made here were:
   a) Be friendly with all people.
   b) Avoid foreign political entanglements and permanent alliances.
   c) Take advantage of our geographic isolation to develop peacefully.

2. This speech contributed a great deal to forming U.S. foreign policy for many years. Its influence, particularly in its isolationist aspects, remained strong in American foreign policy until well into the twentieth century.

3. Although the U.S. government made many temporary alliances, and even considered permanent alliances on a few occasions, it was only after World War II that the U.S. fully accepted a position of international responsibility. Even after World War I, America was unwilling to commit to Woodrow Wilson's League of Nations, but preferred to keep her distance from the rest of the world. The North Atlantic Treaty of 1949 was the first formal alliance between the U.S. and a European nation since the eighteenth century.

4. Answers will vary. The world today is vastly different from Washington's world of two centuries ago. Then, it took weeks to send a message from one nation to another, weeks—or months—to get a response. It would also take months to assemble a fighting force to attack another country. Today, both communication and aggression are available at the touch of a button. A diplomat can travel from Washington to London in a matter of hours. Modern transportation and communication methods have greatly reduced our geographic isolation. As part of a modern world, America is bound to take her part fully in that world, instead of trying to stand alone on the sidelines.

For Further Reading

DeConde, Alexander. *Entangling Alliance: Politics and Diplomacy Under George Washington.* Westport: Greenwood, 1974 (reprint of 1958 edition).

Gilbert, Felix. *To the Farewell Address: Ideas of Early American Foreign Policy.* Princeton: Princeton University Press, 1961.

1798—The Alien and Sedition Acts

The election of 1796 was the first election in which two political parties took part. The Federalist Party was opposed by the newly formed Democratic-Republican Party. The Democratic-Republican Party drew much of its support from new citizens. Two years later, apparently in response to serious foreign problems, Congress passed four acts—the Alien Act, the Alien Enemies Act, the Sedition Act, and the Naturalization Act—which came to be known collectively as the Alien and Sedition Acts. The Alien Act gave the president power to deport any foreigner he regarded as dangerous "to the peace and safety of the United States." The Alien Enemies Act gave the president broad powers to deal with enemy aliens during time of war. The Sedition Act made it a crime to publish anything false or scandalous about the government. Here is an excerpt from the Naturalization Act, which raised the residence requirement for citizenship from five years to fourteen:

Be it enacted . . . , That no alien shall be admitted to become a citizen of the United States, or of any state, unless . . . he shall have declared his intention to become a citizen of the United States, five years, at least, before his admission, and shall, . . . prove, . . . that he has resided within the United States fourteen years, at least. . . . " [The Naturalization Act, June 18, 1798]

—Questions—

1. What do you think the government gave as the reason for this act?

2. What do you think was the real reason for this act?

3. If you had been a recent immigrant to this country in 1798, how would you have reacted to this act? If you had already been a U.S. citizen?

4. Based on your knowledge of the period, what do you think were the short-term effects of the Alien and Sedition Acts? The long-term effects?

5. It has been said that, in times of national crisis or war, governments tend to suspend personal liberties. Can you think of any events in our country in this century which fit that description?

GLOSSARY   **alien**—foreigner
deport—expel from the country

sedition—causing others to rebel against authority

Possible Answers
The Alien and Sedition Acts

A Basic Question: Was the Naturalization Act justified?

1. In 1797, the XYZ Affair brought America close to war. The country was gripped by anti-French fervor. The Federalists claimed that this act—and the other acts of the Alien and Sedition Acts—would help protect the country from enemy aliens in wartime.

2. The Federalist Party hoped that these acts would cripple its political enemies, the Democratic-Republicans. The Republicans had won the support of many radical immigrants to the United States, and were critical of Federalist foreign policy. The XYZ Affair convinced many Federalists that this criticism was disloyal, and the legislation was pushed through Congress, despite the mixed feelings of President John Adams. Since most newcomers joined the Republican Party as soon as they secured their citizenship papers, increasing the residency requirement by nine years would stem, for a time, the increase in the Republican ranks. Also, in light of the anti-French sentiments then prevalent, the Federalists hoped to associate "Republican" and "un-American" in the minds of the people.

3. Answers will vary. The Alien and Sedition Acts drew widespread protest from all over the country, especially from Republicans. Many considered the Sedition Act a violation of the First Amendment, and thus unconstitutional.

4. The Acts had very little direct effect, but their indirect effect was enormous. The Alien Act and the Alien Enemies Act were not enforced. Some twenty-five persons were arrested under the Sedition Act, and ten convicted. Most of them were Republican newspaper editors. However, public reaction against the Acts was widespread, especially among Republicans. The Acts particularly offended recent immigrants and increased their loyalty to the Republicans. Bitter resentment over the Alien and Sedition Acts contributed heavily to the Republican victory in the election of 1800, and the Federalists' loss of standing with the common people of America.

5. Government internment of thousands of Japanese-Americans during World War II is an example.

For Further Reading

Smith, James Morton. *Freedom's Fetters: The Alien and Sedition Laws and American Civil Liberties.* Ithaca: Cornell University Press, 1966.

1803—The Louisiana Purchase

At the end of the French and Indian War in 1763, France gave Spain the Louisiana Territory west of the Mississippi. In 1800, by secret treaty, Spain transferred Louisiana back to France. When President Thomas Jefferson sent Robert Livingston and James Monroe to France to try to buy New Orleans, Napoleon surprised them by offering to sell all of Louisiana for $15 million. This put Jefferson in a difficult position. The president firmly believed that the U.S. should buy Louisiana, but was not sure that the Constitution gave him the power to do so. Opponents of the Louisiana Purchase were quite sure it was unconstitutional. One opponent, Senator Timothy Pickering, explained his opposition to the Senate; the transcription refers to the speaker as "he," although the speech was made in the first person.

"The Constitution, and the laws of the United States made in pursuance thereof, and all treaties made, or which shall be made under the authority of the United States, shall be the supreme law of the land."—But a treaty to be thus obligatory, must not contravene the Constitution, nor contain any stipulations which transcend the powers therein given to the President and Senate. The treaty between the United States and the French Republic, professing to cede Louisiana to the United States, appeared to him to contain such an exceptionable stipulation—a stipulation which cannot be executed by any authority now existing. It is declared in the third article, that "the inhabitants of the ceded territory shall be incorporated in the Union of the United States." But neither the President and Senate, nor the President and Congress, are competent to such an act of incorporation. He believed that our Administration admitted that this incorporation could not be effected without an amendment of the Constitution; and he conceived that this necessary amendment could not be made in the ordinary mode by the concurrence of two-thirds of both Houses of Congress, and the ratification by the Legislatures of three-fourths of the several States. He believed the assent of each individual State to be necessary for the admission of a foreign country as an associate in the Union: in like manner as in a commercial house, the consent of each member would be necessary to admit a new partner into the company; and whether the assent of every State to such an indispensable amendment were attainable, was uncertain. [Transcript of remarks of Sen. Timothy Pickering to the Senate, Nov. 3, 1803]

——Questions——

1. The decision to buy the Louisiana Territory gave rise to a political controversy. Why?

2. List as many reasons as you can think of to explain American interest in buying all or part of the Louisiana Territory.

3. Based on what you already know about this period in U.S. history, think of as many consequences of the Louisiana Purchase as you can.

4. Look at a copy of the Constitution. Can you find anything here to justify purchasing Louisiana?

5. Assume that the Constitution did not specifically allow the president to purchase foreign territories. Suggest several ways Jefferson might be able to make the purchase anyway.

(continued)

1803—The Louisiana Purchase
(continued)

GLOSSARY

amendment—addition to a law or body of laws

associate—partner

attainable—reachable

cede—yield, surrender

competent—legally authorized

conceive—think

concurrence—agreement

contravene—oppose

effect—bring about

exeptionable—unpleasant, objectionable

execute—carry out

incorporation—combining

indispensable—essential

mode—way, manner

obligatory—required

profess—claim

pursuance—carrying out, putting into effect

ratification—approval

stipulation—condition, requirement

supreme—highest, ultimate

thereof—of that

transcend—go beyond

Sample Answers
The Louisiana Purchase

A Basic Question: Was it legal?

1. Jefferson and the Republicans had always favored government by strict observation of the Constitution. The Federalists, on the other hand, had called for a strong national government. In deciding to buy the Louisiana Territory, Jefferson acted against his own principles. Federalists, and some Republicans, objected to Jefferson's broad view of the Constitution.

2. a) France under Napoleon was much stronger than Spain, and might prove an uncomfortable neighbor for the United States. Not only would it be more difficult for the U.S. to expand westward, but Napoleon might want to expand his territory towards the east, onto American soil.

   b) The port of New Orleans was an essential part of the route to markets for western farmers. They could not make a profit by transporting their products over the mountains and bad roads to the east; it was much cheaper to ship goods down the Ohio and Mississippi Rivers for transfer to oceangoing vessels in New Orleans.

   c) According to Jefferson himself, France had always been the "natural friend" of the United States, but taking possession of New Orleans would make her a "natural and habitual enemy" instead. Rather than let a strong power take control of the mouth of the Mississippi, Jefferson was willing to ally himself with Great Britain.

3. a) The Louisiana Purchase doubled the area of the United States.

   b) It increased the nation's natural resources.

   c) It gave the United States control of the Mississippi down to the river's mouth, ending rivalry with Britain, France, and Spain in the Mississippi Valley.

   d) It strengthened national unity by making westerners grateful to the federal government for safeguarding their interests.

   e) It promoted westward expansion.

   f) It forced Jefferson to modify his strict constructionist constitutional theory. Because he recognized the tremendous importance of this territory to the future of the United States, he was willing to relax his position.

   g) It reduced the prestige of the Federalists, who strongly opposed such a step.

   h) The acquisition paved the way for future struggle between North and South over the extension of slavery into the new territories.

   i) It affected Indian policy, as Indians were forced from east of the Mississippi and settled in the Louisiana Territory.

   j) It freed North America from Europe's colonial entanglements and prepared the way for North America's eventual dominance in the Western Hemisphere.

4. Article II, Section 2, Clause 2 of the Constitution names the powers of the president. This article stipulates: "He shall have power, by and with the advice and consent of the Senate, to make treaties, provided two-third of the Senators present concur." This clause, interpreted very broadly, was the basis of the justification for the Louisiana Purchase.

5. Jefferson's first approach was to draw up a constitutional amendment, giving Congress the right to buy foreign territory. When his representatives in France told him that he had to act quickly, as Napoleon might change his mind while Congress and the states were agreeing to an amendment, he put aside his constitutional scruples over the limited powers of the federal government. Under Article II, Section 2, Clause 2 of the Constitution, the president has the power to make treaties. Jefferson used that power to make a treaty to buy the Louisiana Territory— a loose interpretation of the Constitution, but one that Jefferson felt compelled to make in the national interest.

For Further Reading

Brown, Everett S. *Constitutional History of the Louisiana Purchase, 1803-1812.* Seamen, OH: Kelley Publications (reprint of 1920 edition).

Chase, John. *Louisiana Purchase: America's Best Buy.* New York: Pelican.

DeConde, Alexander. *This Affair of Louisiana.* Baton Rouge: Louisiana State University Press, 1979.

1831—Native Americans and the U.S. Government

In 1827, the Cherokee Indians, who occupied extensive lands in northwestern Georgia, set up a government and declared themselves an independent nation. Georgia promptly passed resolutions claiming ownership of all Cherokee territory, and extending the laws of Georgia over the Cherokee Indians. The Cherokee appealed to the Supreme Court to prevent the execution of these laws.

Chief Justice Marshall: . . . If courts were permitted to indulge their sympathies, a case better calculated to excite them can scarcely be imagined. A people, once numerous, powerful, and truly independent, found by our ancestors in the quiet and uncontrolled possession of an ample domain, gradually sinking beneath our superior policy, our arts and our arms, have yielded their lands, by successive treaties, each of which contains a solemn guarantee of the residue, until they retain no more of their formerly extensive territory than is deemed necessary to their comfortable subsistence. To preserve this remnant, the present application is made.

. . . A question of much more difficulty remains. Do the Cherokees constitute a foreign state in the sense of the constitution? The counsel have shown conclusively, that they are not a state of the Union, and have insisted that, individually, they are aliens, not owing allegiance to the United States. An aggregate of aliens composing a state must, they say, be a foreign state; each individual being foreign, the whole must be foreign.

This argument is imposing, but we must examine it more closely, before we yield to it. [*Cherokee Nation* v. *Georgia,* 1831]

——Questions——

1. What does Justice Marshall here define as the central question?

2. If you had been a member of the Supreme Court, what kind of past dealings between the U.S. and Indian nations—treaties, etc.—would you take into account in deciding this case?

3. In your own opinion, should the Cherokee Nation have been treated as a foreign one? Why or why not?

4. The Court declared that Indians were "domestic dependent nations in a state of pupilage." In your own words, explain what this means.

5. What long-term consequences do you think this case has had?

GLOSSARY

aggregate—combination
alien—foreign
ancestor—person from whom one is descended
calculate—design
conclusively—beyond doubt
constitute—make up, form
domain—territory, range
execution—carrying out

imposing—impressive
indulge—yield to
policy—political wisdom
remnant—trace, remainder
residue—remainder
subsistence—living
successive—one after another
sympathy—compassion

Sample Answers
Native Americans and the U.S. Government

A Basic Question: Was the Cherokee Nation a foreign state?

1. He says the central question is whether or not the Cherokee Nation is a foreign state.

2. The court looked at many aspects of past relations between the United States and Indians. In his opinion, Justice Marshall argued that, first, the Indian territory is a part of the United States. Second, in all intercourse with foreign nations, whether made by the U.S. or Indians, Indians were considered to be within the jurisdiction of the United States. The Indians, in their treaties, acknowledged that they were under the protection of the United States, and allowed the United States the exclusive right to regulate trade with them and manage their affairs. The Cherokees in particular were allowed by the treaty of Hopewell, which preceded the constitution, "to send a deputy of their choice, whenever they think fit, to congress." Some tribes made treaties in which they admitted their dependence.

3. Answers will vary.

4. Justice Marshall defined this as follows: "They occupy a territory to which we assert a title independent of their will, which must take effect in point of possession, when their right of possession ceases. Meanwhile, they are in a state of pupilage; their relation to the United States resembles that of a ward to his guardian. They look to our government for protection; rely upon its kindness and its power; appeal to it for relief to their wants; and address the president as their great father. They and their country are considered by foreign nations, as well as by ourselves, as being so completely under the sovereignty of the United States, that any attempt to acquire their lands, or to form a political connection with them would be considered by all as an invasion of our territory and an act of hostility."

5. This case defined the legal relations of the Indians with the United States government: the Indian tribes were not foreign nations but domestic dependent nations in a state of pupilage. This was to have considerable effect on future dealings with the Indians, as the government no longer felt compelled to treat them as independent entities, but as dependent ones.

For Further Reading

Berkhofer, Robert F., Jr. *The White Man's Indian: Images of the American Indian from Columbus to the Present.* New York: Random House, 1979.

Deloria, Vine, Jr. and Clifford M. Lytle. *The Nations Within: The Past and Future of American Indian Sovereignty.* New York: Pantheon, 1984.

Ehle, John. *Trail of Tears: The Rise and Fall of the Cherokee Nation.* Garden City, NY: Doubleday, 1988.

Jackson, Helen H. *A Century of Dishonor: A Sketch of the United States Government's Dealing with Some of the Indian Tribes.* St. Clair Shores, MI: Scholarly Press, 1972 (reprint of 1888 edition).

King, Duane H., ed. *The Cherokee Indian Nation: A Troubled History.* Knoxville: University of Tennessee Press, 1979.

Prucha, Francis P. *The Great Father: The United States Government and the American Indians,* 2 vols. Lincoln, NE: University of Nebraska Press, 1984.

Spicer, Edward H. *A Short History of the Indians of the United States.* Melbourne, FL: Krieger, 1984.

1831—*The Liberator*

Anti-slavery societies were active in the North by the 1780's, but during the years that followed, the solutions they offered to slavery varied widely. At first, public sentiment was generally that slavery would die out by itself. Then, as cotton planting grew in the South, so did the demand for slaves. By the 1830's a new group of radical abolitionists became active. In 1831 one of them, William Lloyd Garrison, founded *The Liberator* in Boston. In his first edition of *The Liberator,* Garrison made this famous pledge:

I am aware, that many object to the severity of my language; but is there not cause for severity? I will be as harsh as truth, and as uncompromising as justice. On this subject, I do not wish to think, or speak, or write, with moderation. No! No! Tell a man whose house is on fire, to give a moderate alarm; tell him to moderately rescue his wife from the hands of the ravisher; tell the mother to gradually extricate her babe from the fire into which it has fallen; —but urge me not to use moderation in a cause like the present. I am in earnest—I will not equivocate—I will not excuse—I will not retreat a single inch—AND I WILL BE HEARD. [*The Liberator,* Vol. I, No. 1, January 1, 1831]

——Questions——

1. Do you think Garrison and *The Liberator* were representative of the abolition movement as a whole?

2. How do you think the southern states reacted to Garrison?

3. Do you think Garrison kept his promise to be heard?

GLOSSARY   **equivocate**—speak uncertainly
extricate—set free, get out
moderation—avoiding extremes

ravisher—rapist
uncompromising—inflexible, rigid

Sample Answers
The Liberator

A Basic Question: Was Garrison right?

1. William Lloyd Garrison was one of the most radical abolitionists. Most abolitionists took a far more moderate position. In fact, some even called Garrison "the Massachusetts madman." While Garrison demanded an immediate and total end to slavery, most moderates were willing to see abolition come gradually.

2. In the South, proslavery newspapers seized the chance to reprint specimens of New England's radicalism to show just how dangerous northern opinions were. By the end of 1831, the Georgia legislature proposed a reward of $5,000 for anyone who would kidnap Garrison and bring him south for trial.

3. Yes, Garrison was certainly heard. *The Liberator* remained in continuous weekly publication until 1865, and always served as a personal sounding board for Garrison's views. Although moderate abolitionists were probably more influential than Garrison, his name is widely identified with the movement, even today.

For Further Reading

Merrill, Walter M. *Against Wind and Tide: A Biography of William Lloyd Garrison.* Boston: Harvard University Press, 1963.

1832—The Spoils System

For many years, the American government operated on the "spoils system." Under this system, jobs and favors were distributed on a political basis rather than according to merit. In some state and provinciaal governments, successful office seekers gave jobs to supporters and eliminated officeholders of the defeated party; later the pattern spread to the federal level. While many presidents were personally honest, and tried to ensure that offices were given to the individuals best suited to fill them, dishonesty was widespread.

The doctrine of "to the victors belong the spoils" was stated baldly by Senator William Marcy, in the course of the debate on the nomination of Martin Van Buren.

It may be, sir, that the politicians of New York are not so fastidious as some gentlemen are, as to disclosing the principles on which they act. They boldly preach what they practice. When they are contending for victory, they avow their intention of enjoying the fruits of it. If they are successful, they claim, as a matter of right, the advantages of success. They see nothing wrong in the rule that to the VICTOR belongs the spoils of the ENEMY. [Speech by Senator William Marcy, 1831]

——Questions——

1. What do you think of the spoils system?

2. Do you agree with Senator Marcy that the successful candidate has the right to reward his or her supporters with positions in government?

3. What steps do you think would have to be taken to reform government and do away with the spoils system?

4. Do you think the spoils system, or a similar system, is still in effect today?

GLOSSARY   **avow**—admit freely   **fastidious**—oversensitive
                  contend—fight   **fruits**—results
                  disclose—make known

Sample Answers
The Spoils System

A Basic Question: Was it fair?

1. Answers will vary.

2. Answers will vary.

3. Progressive reform and the expanded role of the federal government have limited the extent of patronage and the spoils system. The passage of the Civil Service Act of 1883 established a Civil Service Commission to conduct examinations and ruled out political interference in civil service appointments and removals. Political activities of federal employees were limited by the Hatch Act of 1939, which was intended to prevent federal employees from using their power to bribe or intimidate voters. Reformers have established bureaucratic systems to do many of the things formerly carried out by local political party structures. Meanwhile, the expanded role of the federal government has undermined local autonomy by establishing job descriptions and guidelines for federal government jobs. Formal credentials, educational degrees, merit examinations, and bidding statutes have combined to make the distribution of patronage more difficult and less common.

4. Answers will vary.

For Further Reading

Foulke, William D. *Fighting the Spoilsmen: Reminiscences of the Civil Service Reform Movement.* Salem: Ayer, 1974.

1843—Dorothea Dix and Mental Hospital Reform

In 1841, Dorothea Dix, a Massachusetts teacher, visited a jail in East Cambridge, Massachusetts. She found insane persons being kept in an unheated room. Shocked by what she saw, Dix spent the next two years visiting prisons and almshouses across the state. In January 1843 she presented a report on what she found to the state legislature.

. . . I proceed, gentlemen, briefly to call your attention to the present state of insane persons confined within this Commonwealth, in cages, closets, cellars, stalls, pens! Chained, naked, beaten with rods, and lashed into obedience. . . .

Lincoln. A woman in a cage. *Medford.* One idiotic subject chained, and one in a close stall for seventeen years. *Pepperell.* One often doubly chained, hand and foot; another violent; several peaceable now. *Brookfield.* One man caged, comfortable. *Granville.* One often closely confined; now losing the use of his limbs from want of exercise. *Charlemont.* One man caged. *Savoy.* One man caged. *Lenox.* Two in the jail, against whose unfit condition there the jailer protests. . . .

Danvers. . . . Found the mistress, and was conducted to the place which was called "the home" of the forlorn maniac, a young woman. . . . There she stood, clinging to or beating upon the bars of her caged apartment, the contracted size of which afforded space only for increasing accumulations of filth, a foul spectacle. There she stood with naked arms and disheveled hair, the unwashed frame invested with fragments of unclean garments, the air so extremely offensive, though ventilation was afforded on all sides save one, that it was not possible to remain beyond a few moments without retreating for recovery to the outward air. Irritation of body, produced by utter filth and exposure, incited her to the horrid process of tearing off her skin by inches. Her face, neck, and person were thus disfigured to hideousness. She held up a fragment just rent off. To my exclamation of horror, the mistress replied: "Oh, we can't help it. Half the skin is off sometimes. We can do nothing with her; and it makes no difference what she eats, for she consumes her own filth as readily as the food which is brought her." [*Memorial to the Legislature of Massachusetts,* January 1843]

——Questions——

1. How do you think conditions for the insane got to the condition Dix describes in this excerpt?

2. What do you think was Dix's purpose in presenting this report to the legislature?

3. What effects do you think this report might have had?

4. Suggest four ways in which improvements could be made in the conditions described here.

5. In recent years, a great deal of emphasis has been placed on removing the mentally ill from institutions, and returning them to society. Can you see any connections between this deinstitutionalization movement and Dix's work?

(continued)

1843—Dorothea Dix and Mental Hospital Reform
(continued)

GLOSSARY **accumulation**—piling up
confine—imprison
consume—eat
contracted—narrow
disfigure—spoil in appearance
disheveled—untidy
exposure—being open to the weather
filth—dirt
forlorn—wretched, pitiful

foul—dirty
fragment—scrap
hideousness—ugliness
idiotic—mentally deficient
incite—stir up
irritation—soreness, roughness
maniac—mentally ill person
spectacle—sight
want of—lack of

Cases and Controversies in U.S. History

Sample Answers
Dorothea Dix and Mental Hospital Reform

A Basic Question: How should states treat the insane?

1. Answers will vary.

2. When she first became aware of the conditions in jails and almshouses, Dix begged the state legislature to correct these conditions; the legislature did not act. In response, Dix visited more asylums to gather persuasive evidence of the brutal treatment of the insane. Her purpose in presenting this report was to convince the legislature of the need for reform.

3. Through her work, Dix convinced people that the insane were sick, not criminal, and that sick people could not be cured by being put in cages. She finally convinced the Massachusetts legislature to appropriate money to build insane asylums, where her suggestions for the treatment of the insane might be followed. As a result of Dix's work and the work of other reformers, the treatment of the criminal and insane was improved in several ways:
   a) Better facilities were provided in jails and workhouses.
   b) Criminals were no longer whipped.
   c) The death penalty for many crimes was eliminated.
   d) Imprisonment for debt was abolished.
   e) Greater emphasis began to be placed on reforming prisoners rather than punishing them.

4. Answers will vary. Suggestions may include: treating prisoners and the insane in a more humane fashion, making sure they have adequate housing and sanitary facilities, providing medical care, etc.

5. Answers will vary. Some observers see deinstitutionalization as signaling, for many, a return to the kind of conditions described here. In 1955, a total of 560,000 individuals were patients in state or federal mental hospitals. Today, the figure is about 125,000. If the rights of the mentally ill are not carefully safeguarded, it is easy for unscrupulous individuals to take advantage of them. Opponents of deinstitutionalization point out that many of those released from asylums do not have the skills or knowledge to become part of society, and will become increasingly isolated and abused. It is estimated that 30% of the total homeless population suffer from serious mental disorders that make them incapable of making appropriate decisions about where and how they live. Advocates of deinstitutionalization argue that removing these individuals from society is in fact an abrogation of their rights, and that they will be best served by again having the opportunity to function as part of society as a whole.

For Further Reading

Grob, Gerald N. *Mental Institutions in America: Social Policy to 1875.* New York: Free Press, 1973.

Rothman, David J. *The Discovery of the Asylum: Social Order and Disorder in the New Republic* Boston: Little, Brown, 1971.

1846—The Oregon Boundary Dispute

In the early 19th century, Oregon was the vast territory west of the Rockies. It included the present-day states of Oregon, Washington, and Idaho, some of Montana and Wyoming, and much of Canada's province of British Columbia. The territory was originally claimed by France, Spain, Russia, Great Britain, and the United States, but by the 1840's, Great Britain and the United States were the only claimants. In 1818, and again in 1827, the two countries agreed to "joint occupation" of the territory. But in 1844, the Oregon Territory became an issue for many Americans. Here, President James Polk explains his position on the question.

Our title to the country of the Oregon is "clear and unquestionable," and already are our people preparing to perfect that title by occupying it with their wives and children. But eighty years ago our population was confined on the west by the ridge of the Alleghanies. Within that period—within the lifetime, I might say, of some of my hearers—our people, increasing to many millions, have filled the eastern valley of the Mississippi, adventurously ascended the Missouri to its headsprings, and are already engaged in establishing the blessings of self-government in valleys of which the rivers flow to the Pacific. . . . To us belongs the duty of protecting them adequately wherever they may be upon our soil. The jurisdiction of our laws and the benefits of our republican institutions should be extended over them in the distant regions which they have selected for their homes. The increasing facilities of intercourse will easily bring the States, of which the formation in that part of our territory can not be long delayed, within the sphere of our federative Union. [James K. Polk's Inaugural Address, March 4, 1845]

——Questions——

1. In this extract, Polk claims that American title to the Oregon Territory is "clear and unquestionable." What reasons does he give here in support of that title?

2. Based on your knowledge of this period, why do you think the United States wanted to terminate the joint occupation of Oregon, and claim the territory as a part of the U.S.?

3. The United States' claims to the Oregon Territory, especially the area north of the Willamette Valley, were poor. Great Britain had superior claims, as well as a superior navy, and probably could have kept all of Oregon, but in 1846 it agreed to compromise and accept the 49th parallel as a border. Why do you think Britain chose to compromise instead of trying to keep Oregon?

4. Since the U.S. claims to territory north of the Columbia River were weak, Great Britain wanted the northern U.S. boundary set along the Columbia River, while the U.S. continued to demand the 54° 40' line. Both sides eventually agreed to a boundary of 49°. What precedent was there for the 49° compromise?

GLOSSARY   **ascend**—go up, climb
    facility—convenience
    headspring—source

intercourse—interchange, communication
jurisdiction—range of authority
sphere—area of control, domain

Sample Answers
The Oregon Boundary Dispute

A Basic Question: Did joint occupation make sense?

1. The only argument Polk offers in support of the American claim to the Oregon Territory is that many Americans had already moved into the area. In fact, that *was* the main U.S. claim to the area. The British claims were much stronger.

2. An important reason for this sudden access of interest was the growing emigration to Oregon during the 1830's and early 1840's, stimulated in part by glowing reports about the territory's soil and climate and the establishment of overland wagon routes. This emigration was also spurred by the foreclosure of many farms due to the panic of 1837 and the fact that much of the territory east of the Rockies was still being reserved for the use of Native Americans. A second major reason was the proposed annexation of Texas, which raised considerable opposition within the United States. The "All Oregon" claims acted as a kind of political balance to the Texas controversy.

3. Great Britain was willing to compromise for a number of reasons. First, British political leaders had little desire to add to an empire they already thought was overextended. Second, the primary British interest in the area was as a valuable source of furs. By 1846 the Hudson's Bay Company had already trapped out the beaver in southern Oregon, and had moved its principal base to Vancouver Island. In agreeing to the compromise, Britain did not see herself as giving up much of value. Another reason the British may have been willing to compromise lay in their fear that they might eventually lose all of Oregon. Most of the settlers moving into the area were from the United States, not Canada, and Britain had already learned the difficulty of trying to govern Americans against their will.

4. The treaty of 1818 established the precedent of using the 49th parallel to define the border between the United States and Canada. This treaty defined the border for the area from the Lake of the Woods, west of Lake Superior, to the Rocky Mountains. The Oregon Treaty continued the line across to the Pacific Ocean.

For Further Reading

Barrows, William. *Oregon: The Struggle for Possession.* Reprint of 1892 edition. New York: AMS Press.

Dodds, Gordon. *The American Northwest: A History of Washington and Oregon.* Arlington Heights, IL: Forum Press, Inc., 1986.

Dodds, Gordon B. *Oregon: A History.* New York: W.W. Norton & Co., Inc., 1977.

Farnham, Thomas J. *History of the Oregon Territory.* Fairfield, WA: Ye Galleon Press, 1982.

McDuffee, John. *Oregon Crisis.* Fairfield, WA: Ye Galleon Press, 1970.

1846—Henry David Thoreau

In 1846 Henry David Thoreau's residence at Walden was interrupted by a day's imprisonment. He had refused to pay the state's poll tax during the Mexican War on the ground that such a tax abetted the expansionist scheme of southern slave power. His record of the experience was published as *Civil Disobedience* in 1849.

I meet this American government, or its representative, the state government, directly, and face to face, once a year—no more—in the person of its tax-gatherer; this is the only mode in which a man situated as I am necessarily meets it; and it then says distinctly, Recognize me; and the simplest, most effectual, and, in the present posture of affairs, the indispensablest mode of treating with it on this head, or expressing your little satisfaction with and love for it, is to deny it then. My civil neighbor, the tax-gatherer, is the very man I have to deal with,—for it is, after all, with men and not with parchment that I quarrel,—and he has voluntarily chosen to be an agent of the government. How shall he ever know well what he is and does as an officer of the government, or as a man, until he is obliged to consider whether he shall treat me, his neighbor, for whom he has respect, as a neighbor and well-disposed man, or as a maniac and disturber of the peace, and see if he can get over this obstruction to his neighborliness without a ruder and more impetuous thought of speech corresponding with his action. I know this well, and if one thousand, if one hundred, if ten men whom I could name,—if ten *honest* men only,—ay if *one* HONEST man, in this State of Massachusetts, *ceasing to hold slaves*, were actually to withdraw from this copartnership, and be locked up in the county jail therefor, it would be the abolition of slavery in America. For it matters not how small the beginning may seem to be: what is once well done is done forever. [*Civil Disobedience*, 1849]

——Questions——

1. In this excerpt, Thoreau explains why he deliberately disobeyed the law. Can you think of other people in history, either in America or elsewhere, who broke the law in similar ways? What do we call this method of refusing to comply with a law, while accepting the consequences of the refusal?

2. Based on your reading of this excerpt, what can you say about Thoreau's view of individual responsibility and of the relative importance of institutions and principles?

3. Thoreau feared that annexing Texas would lead to an expansion of slavery. Therefore, he refused to pay a poll tax that might provide funds for the Mexican War. What similar arguments do some tax protesters use today?

4. Is there a difference between this kind of tax protest and tax fraud?

GLOSSARY   **abolition**—ending slavery
impetuous—rash, thoughtless
indispensable—essential
obstruction—something that gets in the way

poll tax—fixed tax paid by each person
posture—condition
situated—placed
well-disposed—inclined to be friendly

Sample Answers
Henry David Thoreau

A Basic Question: Did he deserve to go to jail?

1. Mahatma Gandhi in India and the Civil Rights movement in this country in the 1960's both used the technique of passive resistance.

2. In his writing and in his actions, Thoreau emphasized personal ethics and responsibility, urging the individual to follow the dictates of conscience in any conflict with the civil law, and to violate unjust laws to effect their repeal.

3. Some tax protesters object to paying an income tax on the grounds that revenues are used to purchase arms and fund the military. Some protesters make donations, equal to the amount of their tax liability, to peaceful or peace-promoting causes. They do not claim that the government has no right to tax them, merely that they have a right to make some decisions about how their money is to be used. Like Thoreau, these protesters know that they risk being jailed for their refusal to obey the law. They argue that the principle at stake is more important than the threat of punishment.

4. Tax protesters usually do not deny the government's right to tax them, and they report their taxable income; they simply refuse to pay the tax they acknowledge is due. People who commit tax fraud try to lie to the government about the amount they have earned and the amount they owe in order to avoid paying the full amount of tax due.

For Further Reading

Cavell, Stanley. *The Senses of Walden.* Berkeley: North Point Press, 1981.

Eisenhower, John S.D. *So Far From God: The U.S. War With Mexico, 1846-1848.* New York: Random House, 1989.

Harding, Walter, and Michael Meyer. *A Thoreau Handbook.* New York: New York University Press, 1980.

Harding, Walter. *The Days of Henry Thoreau.* New York: Hill & Wang, 1971.

Lebeaux, Richard. *Young Man Thoreau.* Amherst, MA: University of Massachusetts Press, 1977.

Paul, Sherman. *The Shores of America: Thoreau's Inward Exploration.* Champaign, IL: University of Illinois Press, 1972.

Thoreau, Henry David. *Walden* and *Civil Disobedience.* New York: Pocket Books, 1968.

1848—The Seneca Falls Convention

The Seneca Falls Convention was the first women's rights assembly in the United States. It met at Seneca Falls, New York, on July 19–20, 1848. The sixty-eight women and thirty-two men present passed a Declaration of Sentiments, which listed sixteen forms of discrimination against women, including denial of the right to vote and the refusal to give them control of their wages, their own persons, and their children.

The history of mankind is a history of repeated injuries and usurpations on the part of man toward woman, having in direct object the establishment of an absolute tyranny over her. To prove this, let facts be submitted to a candid world.

He has never permitted her to exercise her inalienable right to the elective franchise.

He has compelled her to submit to laws, in the formation of which she had no voice.

He has withheld from her rights which are given to the most ignorant and degraded men—both natives and foreigners.

Having deprived her of this first right of a citizen, the elective franchise, thereby leaving her without representation in the halls of legislation, he has oppressed her on all sides.

He has made her, if married, in the eye of the law, civilly dead.

He has taken from her all right in property, even to the wages she earns.

He has made her, morally, an irresponsible being, as she can commit many crimes with impunity, provided they be done in the presence of her husband. In the covenant of marriage, she is compelled to promise obedience to her husband, he becoming, to all intents and purposes, her master—the law giving him power to deprive her of her liberty, and to administer chastisement.

He has so framed the laws of divorce, as to what shall be the proper causes, and in case of separation, to whom the guardianship of the children shall be given, as to be wholly regardless of the happiness of women—the law, in all cases, going upon a false supposition of the supremacy of man, and giving all power into his hands.

After depriving her of all rights as a married woman, if single, and the owner of property, he has taxed her to support a government which recognizes her only when her property can be made profitable to it.

He has monopolized nearly all the profitable employments, and from those she is permitted to follow, she receives but a scanty remuneration. He closes against her all the avenues to wealth and distinction which he considers most honorable to himself. As a teacher of theology, medicine, or law, she is not known.

He has denied her the facilities for obtaining a thorough education, all colleges being closed against her.

He allows her in Church, as well as State, but a subordinate position, claiming Apostolic authority for her exclusion from the ministry, and, with some exceptions, from any public participation in the affairs of the Church.

He has created a false public sentiment by giving to the world a different code of morals for men and women, by which moral delinquencies which exclude women from society, are not only tolerated, but deemed of little account in man.

He has usurped the prerogative of Jehovah himself, claiming it as his right to assign for her a sphere of action, when that belongs to her conscience and to her God.

He has endeavored, in every way that he could, to destroy her confidence in her

(continued)

1848—The Seneca Falls Convention
(continued)

own powers, to lessen her self-respect and to make her willing to lead a dependent and abject life.

Now, in view of this entire disfranchisement of one-half the people of this country, their social and religious degradation—in view of the unjust laws above mentioned, and because women do feel themselves aggrieved, oppressed, and fraudulently deprived of their most sacred rights, we insist that they have immediate admission to all the rights and privileges which belong to them as citizens of the United States. [The Seneca Falls Declaration of Sentiments, July 19–20, 1848]

——Questions——

1. What document is being imitated here? Why do you think the writers chose that document?

2. In your opinion, which of the grievances listed here is the major one?

3. Which grievance do you think the writers of this document considered the most important? Give reasons for your choice.

4. Choose three of the grievances listed here. How has the situation changed in the century and a half since this list was drawn up? If there is still a cause for a grievance, suggest ways to bring about a change. If the grievance no longer exists, how did the change come about?

GLOSSARY

abject—lacking in self-respect
administer—deal out, give
aggrieve—treat unjustly
apostolic—of the pope
avenue—approach
candid—unbiased, impartial
chastisement—punishment
covenant—formal agreement
degrade—bring shame, disgrace on
disfranchisement—taking rights of citizens away
distinction—honor
elective franchise—vote
endeavor—try
establishment—setting up
exception—exclusion, omission
facilities—means to do something
fraudulently—by trickery, by fraud
guardianship—responsibility
impunity—freedom from punishment

inalienable—cannot be taken away
ministry—position in clergy
monopolize—take all of
oppress—subject to harsh treatment
prerogative—right, privilege
privilege—right, benefit
regardless—heedless, unmindful
remuneration—payment
scanty—small
sentiment—feeling
sphere—area
subordinate—lower, inferior
supposition—theory
supremacy—dominance
theology—study of God
thereby—by that means
thorough—complete
tolerate—allow
tyranny—absolute power
usurp—seize without right or authority

Sample Answers
The Seneca Falls Convention

A Basic Question: Were men tyrannical?

1. The Declaration of Sentiments paralleled the language of the Declaration of Independence. Using the Declaration of Independence as a model underlined their contention that all women, as well as all men, are created equal, and that women are also entitled to "Life, Liberty, and the pursuit of Happiness."

2. Answers will vary.

3. Answers will vary. The refusal of the right to vote is the most likely answer.

4. Answers will vary.

For Further Reading

Berg, Barbara J. *The Remembered Gate: Origins of American Feminism—The Woman and the City, 1800-1860.* New York: Oxford University Press, 1978.

DuBois, Ellen C. *Feminism and Suffrage: The Emergence of an Independent Woman's Movement in America, 1848-1869.* Ithaca: Cornell University Press, 1980.

Griffith, Elisabeth. *In Her Own Right: The Life of Elizabeth Cady Stanton.* New York: Oxford University Press, 1984.

1850—Slavery

Here are two descriptions of slavery, the "peculiar institution" of the southern states.

The master's interest prevents his reducing the slave's allowance or wages in infancy or sickness, for he might lose the slave by so doing. His feeling for his slave never permits him to stint him in old age.

The slaves are all well fed, well clad, have plenty of fuel and are happy. They have no dread of the future—no fear of want. [A Southern defense of slavery]

More than twenty years of my life were consumed in a state of slavery. . . . A master is one (to speak in the vocabulary of the Southern States) who claims and exercises a right of property in the person of a fellow man. This he does with the force of the law and the sanction of Southern religion. The law gives the master absolute power over the slave. He may work him, flog him, hire him out, sell him, and in certain contingencies, *kill* him, with perfect impunity. The slave is a human being, divested of all rights—reduced to the level of a brute—a mere "chattel" in the eye of the law—placed beyond the circle of human brotherhood—cut off from his kind—his name . . . is impiously inserted in a *master's ledger,* with horses, sheep and swine. In law, the slave has no wife, no children, no country, and no home. He can own nothing, possess nothing, acquire nothing, but what must belong to another. To eat the fruit of his own toil, to clothe his person with the work of his own hands, is considered stealing. He toils that another may reap the fruit; he is industrious that another may live in idleness; he eats unbolted meal, that another may ride in ease and splendor abroad; he lives in ignorance, that another may be educated; he is abused, that another may be exalted; he rests his toil-worn limbs on the cold, damp ground, that another may repose on the softest pillow; he is clad in coarse and tattered raiment, that another may be arrayed in purple and fine linen; he is sheltered only by the wretched hovel, that a master may dwell in a magnificent mansion; and to this condition he is bound down as by an arm of iron. [Frederick Douglass lecture in Rochester, New York, December 1, 1850]

——Questions——

1. Frederick Douglass names many of the evils of slavery. Which of them do you think he considered the worst?

2. The first excerpt gives one of several arguments used in the South in defense of slavery. What other proslavery arguments of the time have you seen? Write down as many as you can.

3. Taking an antislavery position, rebut all the arguments you listed above.

4. From Frederick Douglass's description, try to imagine what life would be like if you were a slave. Write a paragraph describing part of your day as a slave.

(continued)

Glossary

abuse—treat badly
array—dress
brute—animal
chattel—piece of property
clad—clothed
consume—use up
contingency—circumstance
divest—deprive, take away
exalt—raise in position
flog—beat, whip
hovel—small, miserable dwelling
impiously—without reverence for God
impunity—freedom from punishment

industrious—hard-working
ledger—account book
magnificent—grand, outstanding
mansion—large, stately house
raiment—clothes
sanction—approval
splendor—grandeur, fine appearance
stint—limit, restrict
tattered—torn, ragged
toil-worn—tired from work
unbolted—not sifted
wretched—poor, shabby

Sample Answers
Slavery

A Basic Question: Was slavery defensible in any way?

1. Answers will vary. Some students may feel that Douglass lays particular emphasis on the evil done to African-Americans by the simple fact that they were not their own masters. Even if slaves were treated decently, they were still given no opportunity to make their own choices and decisions.

2. Answers will vary. Before the development of an aggressive abolition movement, the South tended to apologize for slavery as a "necessary evil." But as they were pressed harder by abolitionist attacks, Southerners began to defend slavery and tout its "good" points. The Southern defense of slavery included the following arguments: 1) Slavery was a natural relationship between whites and blacks, and was socially beneficial to both groups. 2) Slavery was ordained by God and accepted in the Bible. 3) Slavery brought Christianity and the benefits of civilization to Africans. 4) Slaves had more security and were treated more considerately than free workers in Northern factories.

3. Answers will vary.

4. Answers will vary.

For Further Reading

Elliott, E.N., ed. *Cotton Is King and Pro-Slavery Arguments.* Westport: Greenwood (reprint of 1850 edition).

Gutman, Herbert G. *The Black Family in Slavery and Freedom, 1750-1925.* New York: Random House, 1977.

Lester, Julius. *To Be a Slave.* New York: Scholastic, 1986.

Douglass, Frederick. *Narrative of the Life of Frederick Douglass, an American Slave.* New York: Penguin, 1982.

Stampp, Kenneth M. *The Peculiar Institution: Slavery in the Ante-Bellum South.* New York: Knopf, 1956.

1857—The Rights of a Slave

John Emerson, an army surgeon, had taken his slave Scott from Missouri to Illinois, where slavery was prohibited by the Northwest Ordinance, and into the Louisiana Territory, where slavery was forbidden by the Missouri Compromise. Before he died, Emerson took Scott back to Missouri. Scott sued Emerson's widow for his freedom, claiming his time on free soil made him free. The Supreme Court's decision, reached by a seven-to-two vote, was that Scott was not a citizen and thus had no right to sue in the federal courts. Chief Justice Taney made three points in his opinion. First, he observed that Negroes—slave or free—were not included and were not intended to be included in the category of "citizen" as the word was used in the U.S. Constitution. Second, he argued that Scott had not become free by virtue of his residence in a territory covered by the Missouri Compromise, since that legislation was unconstitutional, as it limited the property rights of citizens. Third, whatever may have been the temporary effect of Scott's sojourn in Illinois, Scott had ultimately returned to Missouri, where his status depended on Missouri law.

Chief Justice Taney: . . . It is true, every person, and every class and description of persons, who were at the time of the adoption of the Constitution recognized as citizens in the several States, became also citizens of this new political body; but none other; it was formed by them, and for them and their posterity, but for no one else. . . .

In the opinion of the court, the legislation and histories of the times, and the language used in the Declaration of Independence, show, that neither the class of persons who had been imported as slaves, nor their descendants, whether they had become free or not, were then acknowledged as a part of the people, nor intended to be included in the general words used in that memorable instrument. . . .

And upon a full and careful considera-

tion of the subject, the court is of opinion that, upon the facts stated in the plea in abatement, Dred Scott was not a citizen of Missouri within the meaning of the Constitution of the United States, and not entitled as such to sue in its courts. . . .

. . . It is the consideration of the court that the Act of Congress which prohibited a citizen from holding and owning property of this kind in the territory of the United States north of the line therein mentioned, is not warranted by the Constitution, and is therefore void; and that neither Dred Scott himself, nor any of his family, were made free by being carried into this territory; even if they had been carried there by the owner, with the intention of becoming a permanent resident. . . . [From *Dred Scott* v. *Sanford,* 1857]

——Questions——

1. How do you think North and South reacted to this decision?

2. How do you think abolitionists viewed this decision?

3. What was the significance of the Dred Scott decision?

GLOSSARY **abatement**—legal statement
acknowledge—recognize
adoption—official approval
description—kind or variety
entitle—allow
instrument—document

memorable—remarkable, unforgettable
posterity—a person's descendants
therein—in that place
void—not binding, invalid
warrant—allow, permit

Sample Answers
The Rights of a Slave

A Basic Question: Were slaves citizens?

1 The South was delighted with the court's decision. It seemed to vindicate the Southern point of view and to open the way for the spread of slavery into the territories. The North was shocked and bitter. Antislavery spokesmen accused the Supreme Court of having conspired with Southern slaveholders.

2. This was viewed as a proslavery decision by abolitionists, and the case probably hastened the coming of the Civil War.

3. In its narrow sense, it had no significance. Scott's owner promptly set him free. But in a broad sense, it may have made the Civil War inevitable. The Court was bitterly attacked by antislavery leaders. The result was to make Abraham Lincoln president, and eventually to bring the North and South to war.

For Further Reading

Ehrlich, Walter. *They Have No Rights: Dred Scott's Struggle for Freedom.* Westport: Greenwood, 1979.

Fehrenbacher, Don E. *The Dred Scott Case: Its Significance in American Law and Politics.* New York: Oxford University Press, 1978.

Fehrenbacher, Don E. *Slavery, Law and Politics: The Dred Scott Case in Historical Perspective.* New York: Oxford University Press, 1981.

1868—Impeachment of Andrew Johnson

After Lincoln's assassination in April 1865, Andrew Johnson became president. Johnson soon antagonized the moderate Republicans in Congress. Conflict erupted in February 1868 when, in defiance of the 1867 Tenure of Office Act, Johnson removed Secretary of War Edwin M. Stanton from office, and appointed Lorenzo Thomas in his stead. The House of Representatives quickly moved to impeach Johnson "for high crimes and misdemeanors in office."

Art. X. That said Andrew Johnson, President of the United States, unmindful of the high duties of his office and the dignity and proprieties thereof, and of the harmony and courtesies which ought to exist and be maintained between the executive and legislative branches of the Government of the United States, . . . did attempt to bring into disgrace, ridicule, hatred, contempt, and reproach the Congress of the United States and the several branches thereof, to impair and destroy the regard and respect of all the good people of the United States for the Congress and legislative power thereof (which all offices of the Government ought inviolably to preserve and maintain), and to excite the odium and resentment of all the good people of the United States against Congress and the laws by it duly and constitutionally enacted; and, in pursuance of his said design and intent, . . . [did] make and deliver with a loud voice certain intemperate, inflammatory, and scandalous harangues, and did therein utter loud threats and bitter menaces, as well against Congress as the laws of the United States, duly enacted thereby, amid the cries, jeers, and laughter of the multitudes then assembled and in hearing, which are set forth in the several specifications hereinafter written in substance and effect. . . . [Articles for Impeachment of Andrew Johnson, March 1868]

—Questions—

1. What reasons for impeachment are given in this excerpt?

2. Why do you think Congress moved to impeach the president?

3. In the Senate, thirty-six votes were needed to impeach the president. Seven Republicans voted with the Democrats for acquittal, for a final count of thirty-five for conviction, nineteen for acquittal—one short of the two-thirds majority needed for conviction. Those seven Republicans were politically ruined because of this vote. Why do you think they voted as they did, at the risk of their careers?

4. How would Johnson's conviction have affected the government as a whole?

GLOSSARY

contempt—scorn, low opinion
courtesy—politeness
design—plan
harangue—long, loud speech
harmony—goodwill, accord
hereinafter—in the part after this
impair—weaken
impeach—charge with misconduct
inflammatory—likely to arouse anger or excitement
intemperate—violent
inviolably—regarding as sacred

jeer—mocking shout
legislative—law-making
menace—threat
multitude—crowd
odium—dislike, hatred
propriety—suitability
pursuance—carrying out, putting into effect
reproach—disapproval
scandalous—malicious
specification—statement
substance—essence, gist
thereof—of that

Sample Answers
Impeachment of Andrew Johnson

A Basic Question: Who was in charge?

1. The article stated that, in order to destroy people's respect for Congress, Johnson spoke rudely of Congress in public.

2. During the Civil War, the powers of the executive branch had increased. Not only did the Radical Republicans dislike Johnson, they also wanted to reestablish the position of Congress in government by reducing the importance of the executive and judicial departments.

3. One senator explained his actions in these words: "It is not a party question I am to decide. I must be governed by what my reason and judgment tell me is the truth and the justice and the law of this case. . . . Once set the example of impeaching a President for what, when the excitement of the hour shall have subsided, will be regarded as insufficient causes, and no future President will be safe who happens to differ with a majority of the House and two thirds of the Senate . . . what then becomes of the checks and balances of the Constitution so carefully devised and so vital to its perpetuity? They are all gone." Like the other senators who voted for acquittal, he was considering the larger issues, not merely the concerns of the day.

4. If the president had been convicted on such insubstantial charges, it would have indicated clearly that Congress was the most powerful branch of government in the United States. Congress had already moved to reduce the power of the judicial branch by providing that Supreme Court justices who died or resigned would not be replaced. This led to a shrinking Court. If Congress had been able to convict the president on the grounds given, future presidents would have been wary of coming into conflict with the House of Representatives, for fear they too would be impeached and removed from office.

For Further Reading

Benedict, Michael. *The Impeachment and Trial of Andrew Johnson.* New York: Norton, 1973.

Johnson, Andrew. *Trial of Andrew Johnson, President of the U.S.* (3 vols in 2). New York: Da Capo Press, 1970 (reprint of 1868 edition).

Smith, Gene. *High Crimes and Misdemeanors: The Impeachment and Trial of Andrew Johnson.* New York: McGraw-Hill, 1985.

1895—The Income Tax

A direct tax is a tax paid by the person on whom it is levied. An indirect tax is usually a tax attached to something the person buys—an import tariff on things made abroad, an inventory tax paid by manufacturers or merchants. The Constitution stated that the federal government could impose a direct tax only if the tax was apportioned among the states according to the population of each state. When Congress passed a bill calling for an income tax in 1894, the constitutionality of an income tax was challenged; the Supreme Court found that an income tax was a direct tax, and therefore the federal government could not impose one.

Chief Justice Fuller: . . . The Constitution prohibits any direct tax, unless in proportion to numbers as ascertained by the census, and, in the light of the circumstances to which we have referred, is it not an evasion of that prohibition to hold that a general unapportioned tax, imposed upon all property owners as a body for or in respect of their property, is not direct, in the meaning of the Constitution, because confined to the income therefrom?

Whatever the speculative views of political economists or revenue reformers may be, can it be properly held that the Constitution, taken in its plain and obvious sense, and with due regard to the circumstances attending the formation of the government, authorizes a general unapportioned tax on the products of the farm and the rents of real estate, although imposed merely because of ownership, and with no possible means of escape from payment, as belonging to a totally different class from that which includes the property from whence the income proceeds? [*Pollock* v. *Farmer's Loan and Trust Company*, 1895]

——Questions——

1. Why do you think the men who wrote the Constitution said specifically that the federal government could not levy a direct tax unless it was apportioned among the states?

2. Why do you think Congress passed an income tax law in 1894, despite constitutional restrictions?

3. We do now have an income tax. How do you think this came about?

GLOSSARY **ascertain**—find out
census—official count of population
circumstance—condition
evasion—avoiding, dodging
impose—apply

proportion—balance
speculative—based on theory
unapportioned—not assigned according to proportion

Sample Answers
The Income Tax

A Basic Question: Was an income tax constitutional?

1 Answers will vary. According to Chief Justice Fuller, the nation's founders expected that states would raise money by taxing personal property, while the federal government would raise money by indirect taxes, such as import duties, etc. The restriction was included to be sure that the federal government could only levy a direct tax in case of great need, as during the Civil War.

2. Answers will vary. One reason is that the country changed greatly in the century between the writing of the Constitution and the enactment of an income tax. The nation that emerged from the War of Independence was a small agrarian nation, just thirteen colonies along the eastern seaboard. By 1894, the United States stretched all the way across the continent. Utah, Arizona, Oklahoma and New Mexico had not yet become states, but all were U.S. territories. Industrialization, and the discovery of valuable ore deposits in some states, had changed the face of the economy. With increased domestic production of goods, the amount of goods being imported (and subject to tariffs) was proportionally smaller than one hundred years earlier. At the same time, federal expenses were far greater. The federal government felt that an income tax, which could be graduated to impose a lighter burden on low incomes and a heavier burden on higher ones, would be the fairest way to raise the needed revenue.

3. The Court's decision in this case aroused widespread disaffection. This led eventually to the Sixteenth Amendment, adopted in 1913, which reads, "The Congress shall have the power to lay and collect taxes on incomes, from whatever source derived, without apportionment among the several states, and without regard to any census or enumeration."

For Further Reading

McCarthy, Clarence F. and D. Larry Crumbley. *The Federal Income Tax: Its Sources and Applications,* 1985 edition. Englewood Cliffs, NJ: Prentice-Hall, Inc.

Seidman, J. *Seidman's Legislative History of Federal Income Tax Laws: 1851–1938.* Englewood Cliffs, NJ: Prentice-Hall, Inc., 1938.

Waltman, Jerold L. *Political Origins of the U.S. Income Tax.* Jackson, MS: University Press of Mississippi, 1985.

Witte, John F. *The Politics and Development of the Federal Income Tax.* Madison, WI: University of Wisconsin Press, 1985.

1896—"Separate but Equal"

Homer Plessy was seven-eighths Caucasian and one-eighth black. When he refused to obey a train conductor's order to sit in the car designated for blacks, as Louisiana's segregation laws required, Plessy was arrested. After his conviction Plessy appealed to the U.S. Supreme Court, claiming that the statute was contrary to the 13th and 14th amendments. Here are the opinions of two Supreme Court justices on the case.

Justice Brown: . . . The object of the amendment was undoubtedly to enforce the absolute equality of the two races before the law, but in the nature of things it could not have been intended to abolish distinctions based upon color, or to enforce social, as distinguished from political, equality, or a commingling of the two races upon terms unsatisfactory to either. Laws permitting, and even requiring, their separation in places where they are liable to be brought into contact do not necessarily imply the inferiority of either race to the other, and have been generally, if not universally, recognized as within the competency of the state legislatures in the exercise of their police power. . . . We consider the underlying fallacy of the plaintiff's argument to consist in the assumption that the enforced separation of the two races stamps the colored race with a badge of inferiority. If this be so, it is not by reason of anything found in the act, but solely because the colored race chooses to put that construction upon it.

Justice Harlan: . . . It seems that we have yet, in some of the states, a dominant race, a superior class of citizens, which assumes to regulate the enjoyment of civil rights, common to all citizens, upon the basis of race. . . . The destinies of the two races in this country are indissolubly linked together, and the interests of both require that the common government of all shall not permit the seed of race hate to be planted under the sanction of law. What can more certainly arouse race hate, what more certainly create and perpetuate a feeling of distrust between these races, than state enactments which in fact proceed on the ground that colored citizens are so inferior that they cannot be allowed to sit in public coaches occupied by white citizens? That, as all will admit, is the real meaning of such legislation as was enacted in Louisiana. . . .

I am of opinion that the statute of Louisiana is inconsistent with the personal liberty of citizens, white and black, in that state, and hostile to both the spirit and letter of the Constitution of the United States. [*Plessy* v. *Ferguson,* 1896]

——Questions——

1. One of the opinions given above was the opinion of the Court; the other was the opinion of a judge who disagreed with the majority. Which do you think was which?

2. Read the text of the 14th Amendment to the U.S. Constitution. Which of these opinions comes closest to your interpretation of this amendment?

3. This case established the doctrine of "separate but equal" facilities for whites and African-Americans in this country. In your own words, explain what was meant by "separate but equal."

4. Do you think the "separate but equal" doctrine was a fair way to allocate facilities?

(continued)

1896—"Separate but Equal"
(continued)

GLOSSARY

abolish—put an end to
assumption—idea taken for granted
commingling—mixing
competency—power
construction—interpretation
destiny—fortune, fate
distinguish—set apart
enactment—law
fallacy—false notion

hostile—in opposition
inconsistent—contradictory
indissolubly—permanently
inferiority—lower quality or status
liable—likely
perpetuate—cause to continue
regulate—control
sanction—approval

Sample Answers
"Separate but Equal"

A Basic Question: Can "separate" be "equal"?

1. The first opinion, given by Justice Brown, was the opinion of the majority in this case.

2. Answers will vary. Many students will feel that Justice Harlan's opinion is a more accurate interpretation of this amendment.

3. Answers will vary. Essentially, the "separate but equal" doctrine said that the constitutional rights of African-Americans would be fully upheld so long as they were provided facilities—schools, railway carriages, etc.—equal to those provided for whites. There was no need for them to use the same facilities. Separate schools and dining cars would provide equally for members of both races.

4. Answers will vary. Many students will feel that this was an unfair and unjust system, and that the later judgment in *Brown* v. *Board of Education,* which stated clearly that separate facilities were inherently unequal facilities, was a more equitable decision.

For Further Reading

Woodward, C. Vann. *The Strange Career of Jim Crow.* London: Oxford University Press (third revised edition), 1974.

1903—The Panama Canal

As far back as the early sixteenth century, people had talked of an artificial waterway connecting the Atlantic and the Pacific. The technology to make such a canal possible was not developed until the late 1800's. In 1902, after a French company had tried and failed to construct a canal through Panama, the United States bought out the French interests and began talks with Colombia for the rights to build a canal. These talks failed. But almost immediately a revolution—supported by the Roosevelt administration—broke out in Panama. On November 4, 1903, the new government was installed. It was recognized by the United States on November 6, and on November 18, the Hay-Bunau-Varilla Treaty was signed.

The Republic of Panama grants to the United States in perpetuity the use, occupation and control of a zone of land and land under water for the construction, maintenance, operation, sanitation and protection of said Canal of the width of ten miles extending to the distance of five miles on each side of the center line of the route of the canal to be constructed; the said zone beginning in the Caribbean Sea, three marine miles from mean low water mark, and extending to and across the Isthmus of Panama into the Pacific Ocean to a distance of three marine miles from mean low water mark. . . . [The Hay-Bunau-Varilla Treaty, November 18, 1903]

——Questions——

1. Why, do you think, is a canal across Central America important to the United States? Give at least two reasons.

2. As early as 1850, the United States and Great Britain had agreed that, if a canal were ever built, they would control it together. By 1901 the United States had changed its mind, and asked Great Britain to abandon its rights to share in the building and management of a canal. Why might American thinking have changed?

3. Some time after the revolt in Panama Theodore Roosevelt said, "No one connected with the American government had any part in preparing, inciting, or encouraging the revolution." However, on another occasion he said, "If I had followed traditional conservative methods I would have submitted a dignified State paper of probably 200 pages to Congress and the debates on it would have been going on yet; but I took the Canal Zone and let Congress debate; and while the debate goes on the Canal does also." Can you reconcile these two statements? Which do you think comes closer to being the truth?

4. Does the United States have the right to interfere with other countries in order to promote projects like the Panama Canal? Write down as many arguments as you can think of both for and against U.S. actions in Panama.

GLOSSARY **in perpetuity**—forever

Sample Answers
The Panama Canal

A Basic Question: What rights did the U.S. have in Panama?

1. Both economic and military factors contributed to U.S. interest in a canal.
    a) With possessions in both the Caribbean and the Pacific, the United States needed to be able to move her navy quickly from ocean to ocean. This was made evident during the Spanish-American War, when the public imagination was caught by the voyage of the U.S. battleship *Oregon* from California waters around South America to reach and strengthen the Atlantic fleet. A canal across Central America would have shortened its trip by 7,000 miles! b) Manufacturers and farmers eager for cheap transportation and new outlets for their products at home and abroad pressed for a canal.

2. Americans had concluded, especially in the light of the Spanish-American War, that the canal was so important to the United States, this country must have exclusive control over it.

3. Answers will vary.

4. Answers will vary.

For Further Reading

Bennett, I. *History of the Panama Canal.* New York: Gordon Press, 1976.

Crane, Philip M. *Surrender in Panama: The Case Against the Treaty.* Ottawa, IL: Green Hill, 1978.

DuVal, Miles P. *Cadiz to Cathay: The Story of the Long Diplomatic Struggle for the Panama Canal.* Westport: Greenwood, 1968 (reprint of 1947 edition).

LaFeber, Walton. *The Panama Canal: The Crisis in Historical Perspective.* New York: Oxford University Press, 1978.

McCullough, David. *The Path Between the Seas: The Creation of the Panama Canal, 1870-1914.* New York: Simon and Shuster, 1977.

Williams, Mary W. *Anglo-American Isthmian Diplomacy, 1815-1915.* Magnolia, MA: Peter Smith, 1965.

1905—Tammany Hall

During the second half of the nineteenth century and the early years of the twentieth, city and even state politics in New York were often dominated by an organization called Tammany Hall. Tammany organized voters and elected its candidates so efficiently that its methods were called "machine politics." From the 1860's, Tammany was led by powerful political bosses. Machine politics were frequently associated with corruption, and some bosses became notorious for looting city treasuries. In 1905, William Riordon transcribed conversations he held with George Washington Plunkitt, a ward boss under the Tammany system. Plunkitt speaks:

Everybody is talkin' these days about Tammany men growin' rich on graft, but nobody thinks of drawin' the distinction between honest graft and dishonest graft. There's all the difference in the world between the two. Yes, many of our men have grown rich in politics. I have myself. I've made a big fortune out of the game, and I'm gettin' richer every day, but I've not gone in for dishonest graft—blackmailin' gamblers, saloonkeepers, disorderly people, etc.—and neither has any of the men who have made big fortunes in politics.

There's an honest graft, and I'm an example of how it works. I might sum up the whole thing by sayin': "I seen my opportunities and I took 'em."

Just let me explain by examples. My party's in power in the city, and it's goin' to undertake a lot of public improvements. Well, I'm tipped off, say, that they're going to lay out a new park at a certain place.

I see my opportunity and I take it. I go to that place and I buy up all the land I can in the neighborhood. Then the board of this or that makes its plan public, and there is a rush to get my land, which nobody cared particular for before.

Ain't it perfectly honest to charge a good price and make a profit on my investment and foresight? Of course, it is. Well, that's honest graft. . . .

Now, in conclusion, I want to say that I don't own a dishonest dollar. If my worst enemy was given the job of writin' my epitaph when I'm gone, he couldn't do more than write:

"George W. Plunkitt. He Seen His Opportunities, and He Took 'Em." [*Plunkitt of Tammany Hall*, edited by William L. Riordan, 1905]

——Questions——

1. What does this excerpt tell you about the Tammany Hall view of government and corruption?

2. What kind of reforms would be needed to reduce this kind of corruption?

3. Do you think this kind of corruption is still widely found in city and state governments?

GLOSSARY   epitaph—inscription on a tombstone in memory of person buried there

graft—using one's political position for dishonest gain

77   *Cases and Controversies in U.S. History*

Sample Answers
Tammany Hall

A Basic Question: Can graft be justified?

1. The speaker here obviously does not think that it is possible to have a non-corrupt government. He sees the choice as being between two different types of corruption, the type he practices and the type that involves "blackmailin' gamblers, saloonkeepers, disorderly people, etc." For many large American cities at the close of the nineteenth century, these were, in fact, the choices to be made in government.

2. Answers will vary. The civil service reforms of the late nineteenth and early twentieth century aimed to reduce many abuses, including the kind of corruption described here. One aspect of these reforms was the introduction of civil service exams as a prerequisite of employment. Another was a bureaucratic hierarchy, which involved more supervision of individuals, making it more difficult for any one person to abuse power excessively.

3. Answers will vary.

For Further Reading

Myers, Gustavus. *History of Tammany Hall.* New York: B. Franklin, 1967 (reprint of 1917 edition).

Riordon, William L. *Plunkitt of Tammany Hall.* New York: Dutton, 1963.

1918—The League of Nations

In his address to Congress on January 8, 1918, Woodrow Wilson outlined the steps the United States and its allies would have to take in order to ensure a postwar world "made fit to live in." The fourteenth point of this plan was the idea of a league of nations. When the League of Nations was established on January 10, 1920, it disappointed some of its early supporters. The Covenant, which was the basis for the league's operation, was included in the Treaty of Versailles imposed on defeated Germany. This made it look as if the league was a tool for the victors to use against their former enemies. The U.S. Senate refused to ratify the peace treaty and, in a blow to President Wilson, also kept the country out of the League.

Gentlemen of the Congress: . . .

We entered this war because violations of right had occurred which touched us to the quick and made the life of our own people impossible unless they were corrected and the world secured once for all against their recurrence. What we demand in this war, therefore, is nothing peculiar to ourselves. It is that the world be made fit and safe to live in; and particularly that it be made safe for every peace-loving nation which, like our own, wishes to live its own life, determine its own institutions, be assured of justice and fair dealing by the other peoples of the world as against force and selfish aggression. All the peoples of the world are in effect partners in this interest, and for our own part we see very clearly that unless justice be done to others it will not be done to us. . . .

XIV. A general association of nations must be formed under specific covenants for the purpose of affording mutual guarantees of political independence and territorial integrity to great and small states alike.

In regard to these essential rectifications of wrong and assertions of right we feel ourselves to be intimate partners of all the governments and peoples associated together against the Imperialists. We cannot be separated in interest or divided in purpose. We stand together until the end. [Woodrow Wilson's Address to Congress, January 8, 1918]

—Questions—

1. If you had been a senator in 1918, would you have voted in favor of the League of Nations, or against? Give reasons for your decision.

2. Why do you think the U.S. refused to join the League of Nations?

3. How might the League of Nations have been different if America had joined it?

GLOSSARY   **covenant**—agreement   **rectification**—setting right, correcting
integrity—completeness, unity

Sample Answers
The League of Nations

A Basic Question: Should the U.S. have joined?

1. Answers will vary.

2. Among the reasons given for refusing to join the League were:
   a) The League was an "entangling alliance," which Washington, Jefferson, and Monroe had all warned against.
   b) Some Americans opposed the League because they opposed the Treaty of Versailles, of which the League covenant was a part.
   c) Joining the League of Nations might have forced us to decrease our tariff, increase our immigration, or cancel the Monroe Doctrine.
   d) The League would have threatened the Constitution by taking away from Congress the power to declare war.

3. Among the many problems that led to the termination of the League of Nations were its lack of credibility and lack of police power. Both of these could have been improved if the United States had decided to join. The lack of credibility stemmed, in part, from the fact that the League was conceived by an American, but his own country refused to take part in it. This left other nations with the feeling that Wilson and the U.S. had never intended to be part of the League, and that in some way there was an advantage to be gained by not joining the League. United States membership would also have given the League greater power to enforce its decisions, as the United States was far less debilitated by the war than the other major world powers. The League's inability to take a strong stand, first in Manchuria and then in Ethiopia, led to its final dissolution.

For Further Reading

Kuehl, Warren F. *Seeking World Order: The United States and International Organization to 1920.* Nashville: Vanderbilt University Press, 1969.

Stone, Ralph A. *The Irreconcilables: The Fight Against the League of Nations.* New York: Norton, 1973.

Walworth, Arthur. *Wilson and His Peacemakers: The Paris Peace Conference, 1919.* New York: Norton, 1985.

Widenor, William C. *Henry Cabot Lodge and the Search for an American Foreign Policy.* Berkeley: University of California Press, 1983.

UNIT 34
1921—Sacco and Vanzetti

In 1921, two Italian-born anarchists, Nicola Sacco and Bartolomeo Vanzetti, were convicted of murdering a paymaster and guard in Braintree, Massachusetts. Sympathizers claimed that the men were convicted for their political beliefs. In 1926, the defense tried to reopen the case after hearing testimony that the murders were committed by a criminal gang. The judge refused to call for a new trial. In August, 1927, Sacco and Vanzetti died in the electric chair. In 1977 the governor of Massachusetts reviewed the case and declared that any "disgrace should be forever removed from their names." Vanzetti's last statement in court was a moving protestation of his innocence:

Yes. What I say is that I am innocent. . . . Everybody that knows these two arms knows very well that I did not need to go in between the street and kill a man to take the money. I can live with my two arms and live well. . . . Not only have I struggled all my life to eliminate crimes that the official law and the official moral condemns, but also the crime that the official moral and the official law sanctions and sanctifies,—the exploitation and the oppression of the man by the man, and if there is a reason why I am here as a guilty man, if there is a reason why you in a few minutes can doom me, it is this reason and none else. . . .

We were tried during a time that has now passed into history. I mean by that, a time when there was hysteria of resentment and hate against the people of our principles, against the foreigner, against slackers. . . .

This is what I say: I would not wish to a dog or to a snake, to the most low and misfortunate creature on the earth—I would not wish to any of them what I have had to suffer for things that I am not guilty of. But my conviction is that I have suffered for things that I am guilty of. I am suffering because I am a radical and indeed I am a radical; I have suffered because I was an Italian, and indeed I am an Italian; I have suffered more for my family and for my beloved than for myself; but I am so convinced to be right that if you could execute me two times, and if I could be reborn two other times, I would live again to do what I have done already. I have finished. Thank you. [Bartolomeo Vanzetti's last statement in court, April 9, 1927]

——Questions——

1. In Vanzetti's opinion, why has he been charged and convicted?

2. What is Vanzetti referring to when he says, "We were tried during a time that has now passed into history"?

3. Based solely on what you have read here, do you think Vanzetti was guilty or innocent? On what do you base your belief?

GLOSSARY   exploitation—taking advantage of
hysteria—extreme fear

sanctify—make sacred
sanction—authorize

Sample Answers
Sacco and Vanzetti

A Basic Question: Were they innocent?

1. He feels he was convicted only because he is Italian and an anarchist.

2. In the early 1920's, in the wake of the war and the rise of the Communist Soviet regime, the country was dominated by a "Red Scare." Radicalism in any form was seen as dangerous, un-American. Sacco and Vanzetti were tried when the Red Scare was at its height, and their admitted radical politics told against them.

3. Answers will vary. Students may be struck by the eloquence and sincerity of Vanzetti's words and argue in favor of his innocence from his speech.

For Further Reading

Jackson, Brian. *The Black Flag: A Look Back at the Strange Case of Nicola Sacco and Bartolomeo Vanzetti.* Boston: Routledge & Kegan, 1981.

Joughin, Louis, and E. M. Morgan. *The Legacy of Sacco and Vanzetti.* Princeton: Princeton University Press, 1978.

Montgomery, Robert H. *Sacco-Vanzetti.* Belmont, MA: Western Islands, 1965.

Young, William, and David E. Kaiser. *Postmortem: New Evidence in the Case of Sacco and Vanzetti.* Amherst: University of Massachusetts Press, 1985.

1937—Court-Packing

Toward the end of Franklin D. Roosevelt's first administration, the Supreme Court began to declare important New Deal legislation unconstitutional. In 1937 Roosevelt introduced legislation designed to change the makeup of the Court. Roosevelt's proposal would empower the president to appoint a new member whenever an incumbent justice, who had been acting as a judge for at least ten years, failed to retire at the age of seventy; most of the conservatives on the Supreme Court were already over seventy. The maximum number of justices would be set at fifteen, six more than the court then consisted of. Here is part of the president's explanation of this bill:

When I commenced to review the situation with the problem squarely before me, I came by a process of elimination to the conclusion that short of amendments the only method which was clearly constitutional, and would at the same time carry out other much-needed reforms, was to infuse new blood into all our courts. We must have men worthy and equipped to carry out impartial justice. But at the same time we must have judges who will bring to the courts a present-day sense of the Constitution—judges who will retain in the courts the judicial functions of a court and reject the legislative powers which the courts have today assumed. . . .

What is my proposal? It is simply this: Whenever a judge or justice of any Federal court has reached the age of 70 and does not avail himself of the opportunity to retire on a pension, a new member shall be appointed by the President then in office, with the approval, as required by the Constitution, of the Senate of the United States.

That plan has two chief purposes: By bringing into the judicial system a steady and continuing stream of new and younger blood, I hope, first, to make the administration of all Federal justice speedier and therefore less costly; secondly, to bring to the decision of social and economic problems younger men who have had personal experience and contact with modern facts and circumstances under which average men have to live and work. This plan will save our National Constitution from hardening of the judicial arteries. [Franklin Delano Roosevelt's Address, March 9, 1937]

——Questions——

1. What does Roosevelt give here as his reasons for presenting this bill?

2. What do you think were his real reasons?

3. What flaws can you find in his arguments?

4. The president's bill was referred to the Committee on the Judiciary. How do you think they responded to it?

GLOSSARY amendment—addition to a law or a body of laws

elimination—rejection
impartial—not favoring either side

Sample Answers
Court-Packing

A Basic Question: Was Roosevelt right?

1. He argues that changing the courts as he suggests will make the courts more efficient. He claims that his bill will: 1) bring a steady stream of new blood into the judicial system; 2) make trials faster, and therefore less costly; 3) get younger, experienced men onto the courts.

2. Many of the Supreme Court decisions that went against New Deal legislation were very close—four justices in favor of the laws, five against. If Roosevelt were able to appoint a few justices more favorable to his programs, he might be able to get the majority on his side, instead of against him.

3. Roosevelt's main arguments were that his bill would bring "a steady and continuing stream of new and younger blood" into the judicial system, especially "younger men who have had personal experience and contact with modern facts and circumstances." However, his bill could not ensure any of these things. In the first place, a maximum limit of fifteen justices was included in the bill. If, in 1937, all nine Supreme Court justices were seventy, the president could not appoint more than six new justices. And if these were all long-lived individuals, the same fifteen justices could still be on the court twenty years later, in 1957. Thus, the words "steady" and "continuous" could hardly be used to describe the introduction of "new blood."

   Secondly, the bill could not in any way ensure that the new justices appointed would be either young or experienced. The president could appoint, and the Senate confirm, justices of any age and experience. The Court could conceivably be filled with old, inexperienced judges; no provisions in the bill would prevent it. Also, the bill itself was in a way designed to discriminate against experienced justices. It specified that new justices could be appointed only when a judge had "attained the age of seventy years and has held a commission or commissions as judge of any such court or courts at least ten years." In other words, if a judge with only one or two years experience on the court reached the age of seventy, the president could not appoint a new justice; this was only an option when a judge with a decade or more of experience reached that age.

4. The Committee on the Judiciary recommended against passing the bill.

For Further Reading

Pusey, Merlo J. *The Supreme Court Crisis.* New York: Da Capo Press, 1972 (reprint of 1937 edition).

1939—Roosevelt's Appeals for Peace in Europe

During the period from the Munich Conference of September, 1938, to the outbreak of war in September, 1939, President Franklin D. Roosevelt tried to convince the European powers, especially Germany and Italy, to maintain peace.

You realize I am sure that throughout the world hundreds of millions of human beings are living today in constant fear of a new war or even a series of wars.

. . . Three nations in Europe and one in Africa have seen their independent existence terminated. A vast territory in another independent nation of the Far East has been occupied by a neighboring state. Reports, which we trust are not true, insist that further acts of aggression are contemplated against still other independent nations. Plainly the world is moving toward the moment when this situation must end in catastrophe unless a more rational way of guiding events is found.

. . . I am convinced that the cause of world peace would be greatly advanced if the nations of the world were to obtain a frank statement relating to the present and future policy of governments.

. . . Are you willing to give assurance that your armed forces will not attack or invade the territory or possessions of the following independent nations: Finland, Estonia, Latvia, Lithuania, Sweden, Norway, Denmark, The Netherlands, Belgium, Great Britain and Ireland, France, Portugal, Spain, Switzerland, Liechtenstein, Luxemburg, Poland, Hungary, Rumania, Yugoslavia, Russia, Bulgaria, Greece, Turkey, Iraq, the Arabias, Syria, Palestine, Egypt and Iran.

Such an assurance clearly must apply not only to the present day but also to a future sufficiently long to give every opportunity to work by peaceful methods for a more permanent peace. I therefore suggest that you construe the word "future" to apply to a minimum period of assured non-aggression—ten years at the least—a quarter of a century, if we dare look that far ahead.

If such assurance is given by your Government, I will immediately transmit it to the governments of the nations I have named and I will simultaneously inquire whether, as I am reasonably sure, each of the nations enumerated above will in turn give like assurance for transmission to you. . . . [Letter from F.D. Roosevelt to Adolf Hitler, April 14, 1939]

—Questions—

1. What events are being referred to in the second paragraph of this excerpt?

2. If Hitler had responded to this letter with the assurances Roosevelt requested, how do you think the countries named would have reacted? How *should* they have reacted?

3. With the benefit of hindsight, we can easily see that war with Germany was inevitable, and that Roosevelt would have been wiser to prepare for war than to try to prevent it by diplomatic means. Why do you think Roosevelt and other world leaders did not seem to accept this fact?

GLOSSARY **contemplate**—consider
enumerate—name, list

non-aggression—not attacking
terminate—end

85 *Cases and Controversies in U.S. History*

Sample Answers
Roosevelt's Appeals for Peace in Europe

A Basic Question: Was peace possible?

1. Japan invaded Manchuria in 1931, and moved on China in 1937. Italy annexed Ethiopia in 1936. In March of 1938 Hitler annexed Austria, and in September negotiated for the Sudetenland. In March, 1939, he invaded what was left of Czechoslovakia.

2. Answers will vary. Students may answer that none of the countries named, especially Poland, Denmark, Hungary, Switzerland, Belgium, Luxemburg, France, and The Netherlands, should have taken any assurances from Hitler as proof of his intentions, and should have been making preparations for invasion.

3. Western democracies pursued a policy of appeasement in the face of German, Italian, and Japanese aggression. They followed this policy for three reasons. First, with the memory of the horrors of World War I fresh in their minds, many in the West simply could not believe that any nation would act to begin another war. Second, many diplomats felt that Germany had been mistreated in the Versailles Treaty. They felt that the Germans had legitimate grievances that should be acknowledged and addressed. And finally, they were strongly anti-communist. They believed that by helping Germany to restore its military and economic power they were helping stop the westward advance of Soviet communism.

For Further Reading

Cole, Wayne S. *Roosevelt and the Isolationists, 1932-1945.* Lincoln, NE: University of Nebraska Press, 1983.

Dallek, Robert. *Franklin D. Roosevelt and American Foreign Policy, 1932-1945.* New York: Oxford University Press, 1979.

Divine, Robert A. *Roosevelt and World War Two.* New York: Penguin, 1970.

Hoggan, David L. *President Roosevelt and the Origins of the 1939 War.* New York: Revisionist Press, 1983.

Kimball, Warren F. *Franklin D. Roosevelt and the World Crisis, 1937-1945.* Raytheon, MA: Heath, 1974.

1940—Due Process of Law

This case was brought to the Supreme Court by four young men. The four had been convicted of the murder of an elderly man, and sentenced to death.

Justice Black. . . . The record shows—About nine o'clock on the night of Saturday, May 13, 1933, Robert Darcy, an elderly white man, was robbed and murdered in Pompano, Florida. . . . Between 9:30 and 10 o'clock after the murder, petitioner Charlie Davis was arrested, and within the next twenty-four hours from twenty-five to forty negroes living in the community, including petitioners Williamson, Chambers and Woodward, were arrested without warrants and confined in the Broward County jail, at Fort Lauderdale. . . .

It is clear from the evidence of both the State and petitioners that from Sunday, May 14, to Saturday, May 20, the thirty or forty negro suspects were subjected to questioning and cross questioning. From the afternoon of Saturday, May 20, until sunrise of the 21st, petitioners and possibly one or two others underwent persistent and repeated questioning.

So far as appears, the prisoners at no time during the week were permitted to see or confer with counsel or a single friend or relative. When carried singly from his cell and subjected to questioning, each found himself, a single prisoner, surrounded in a fourth floor jail room by four to ten men, the county sheriff, his deputies, a convict guard, and other white officers and citizens of the community.

. . . by Saturday, May 20th, five days of continued questioning had elicited no confession. Admittedly, a concentration of effort—directed against a small number of prisoners including petitioners—on the part of the questioners, principally the sheriff and Williams, the convict guard, began about 3:30 that Saturday afternoon. From that hour on, with only short intervals for food and rest for the questioners—"They all stayed up all night." "They bring one of them at a time backwards and forwards . . . until they confessed."

After one week's constant denial of all guilt, petitioners "broke."

Just before sunrise, the State officials got something "worthwhile" from petitioners which the State's attorney would "want". . . . These are the confessions utilized by the State to obtain the judgments upon which petitioners were sentenced to death. No formal charges had been brought before the confession. [*Chambers* v. *Florida,* 1940]

——Questions——

1. List every infringement of an individual's rights you see in this excerpt.

2. Based on what you know of U.S. civil rights, what do you think was the basis of the case the four convicted men brought?

3. If you had been on the Supreme Court, how would you have decided this case?

GLOSSARY   **persistent**—continuous   **utilize**—use
                   petitioner—person bringing an action

Sample Answers
Due Process of Law

A Basic Question: What is due process?

1. a) The suspects were arrested on suspicion without warrants. b) The suspects were not permitted to contact a lawyer, or any other person outside the jail. c) The suspects were submitted to continuous questioning that amounted to compulsion. d) The setting in which the confessions were elicited was manifestly unfair and prejudiced.

2. The Fourteenth Amendment to the U.S. Constitution says that no state shall "deprive any person of life, liberty, or property, without due process of law; nor deny to any person within its jurisdiction the equal protection of the laws." The question in *Chambers* v. *Florida* was whether the proceedings in this case, which resulted in death sentences for four young black men, failed to safeguard that due process of law.

3. Answers may vary. The Supreme Court found in favor of the petitioners, saying that "to permit human lives to be forfeited upon confessions thus obtained would make of the constitutional requirement of due process of law a meaningless symbol."

For Further Reading

Bodenhamer, David J. *Fair Trial: Rights of the Accused in American History*. New York: Oxford University Press, 1991.

Pennock, J. Roland and John W. Chapman, eds. *Due Process*. New York: New York University Press, 1977.

1940—The Gobitis Case

The Gobitis children were expelled from the public schools of Minersville, Pennsylvania, for refusing to salute the American flag as required by the local board of education. They were members of the Watch Tower Bible and Tract Society, the "Jehovah's Witnesses," which held that such a salute was contrary to scripture. Their father, Walter Gobitis, brought suit against the school board. He wanted the board to allow his children to attend public school without taking part in the flag-salute ceremony. The district court and the circuit court both decided in Gobitis's favor. The school board appealed to the Supreme Court.

Justice Frankfurter. . . . The Gobitis family are affiliated with "Jehovah's Witnesses," for whom the Bible as the Word of God is the supreme authority. The children had been brought up conscientiously to believe that such a gesture of respect for the flag was forbidden by command of scripture. . . .

Centuries of strife over the erection of particular dogma as exclusive or all-comprehending faiths led to the inclusion of a guarantee for religious freedom in the Bill of Rights. The First Amendment, and the Fourteenth through its absorption of the First, sought to guard against repetition of those bitter religious struggles by prohibiting the establishment of a state religion and by securing to every sect the free exercise of its faith. So pervasive is the acceptance of this precious right that its scope is brought into question, as here, only when the conscience of individuals collides with the felt necessities of society.

Certainly the affirmative pursuit of one's convictions about the ultimate mystery of the universe and man's relation to it is placed beyond the reach of law. Government may not interfere with organized or individual expression of belief or disbelief. Propagation of belief—or even of disbelief in the supernatural—is protected, whether in church or chapel, mosque or synagogue, tabernacle or meetinghouse. Likewise the Constitution assures generous immunity to the individual from imposition of penalties for offending, in the course of his own religious activities, the religious views of others, be they a minority or those who are dominant in government.

But the manifold character of man's relations may bring his conception of religious duty into conflict with the secular interests of his fellow-men. When does the constitutional guarantee compel exemption from doing what society thinks necessary for the promotion of some great common end, or from a penalty for conduct which appears dangerous to the general good? [*Minersville School District* v. *Gobitis*, 1940]

——Questions——

1. Think of as many arguments as you can in favor of Mr. Gobitis's case.

2. Think of as many arguments as you can in favor of the school board's position.

3. What issues were presented in this case?

4. If you had been a Supreme Court justice deciding this case, how would you have voted?

GLOSSARY
absorption—inclusion
affiliate—join, associate
all-comprehending—including everything
conception—idea
conscientiously—carefully, seriously
dogma—belief, idea
immunity—freedom from penalty
Jehovah's Witness—religious sect

manifold—of many kinds, varied
mosque—Muslim house of worship
pervasive—found everywhere
propagation—spreading
secular—not related to religion
strife—conflict, struggle
synagogue—Jewish house of worship
tabernacle—place of worship

Sample Answers
The Gobitis Case

A Basic Question: How powerful is conscience?

1. Answers will vary.

2. Answers will vary.

3. Issues include: the rights of the individual as opposed to the needs of society; the right of the individual to freedom of worship; the right to speak out privately and publicly; the jurisdiction of the courts.

4. Answers will vary. The Supreme Court actually found in favor of the School Board, and stated that the Board was within its rights to insist on the flag-salute ceremony as a prerequisite for attending school. However, a similar suit was brought in West Virginia in 1943, *West Va. State Bd.* v. *Barnette,* in which the Supreme Court reversed its position and overruled the decision in the Gobitis case.

For Further Reading

Stroup, H.H. *The Jehovah's Witnesses.* New York: Columbia University Press, 1945.

Commager, H.S. *Majority Rule and Minority Rights.* Gloucester, MA: Peter Smith, 1958.

1942—Japanese-American Internment

On the whole, there were fewer violations and restrictions of civil liberties during World War II than in other wars. Conscientious objectors and pacifists were treated leniently and there was a minimum of discrimination against minorities. Rights and opportunities in industry for African-Americans were extended. The one notable exception was the forced removal of some 112,000 Japanese-Americans, many of them U.S. citizens, from the West Coast, and their confinement in huge army-run relocation centers. Some Japanese-Americans, claiming their rights as citizens, refused to comply with the order to relocate. In 1943, one Japanese-American man appealed his conviction for failing to report to the Civil Control Station and failing to obey a curfew order that applied only to Americans of Japanese descent.

Justice Stone: . . . Appellant does not deny that he knowingly failed to obey the curfew order. . . . His contentions are only that Congress unconstitutionally delegated its legislative power to the military commander by authorizing him to impose the challenged regulation, and that, even if the regulation were in other respects lawfully authorized, the Fifth Amendment prohibits the discrimination made between citizens of Japanese descent and those of other ancestry. . . . As the curfew was made applicable to citizens residing in the area only if they were of Japanese ancestry, our inquiry must be whether in the light of all the facts and circumstances there was any substantial basis for the conclusion, in which Congress and the military commander united, that the curfew as applied was a protective measure necessary to meet the threat of sabotage and espionage which would substantially affect the war effort and which might reasonably be expected to aid a threatened enemy invasion. [*Hirabayashi* v. *United States*, 1943]

——Questions——

1. Given your knowledge of the U.S. Constitution and civil rights, what do you think was the verdict of the court in this case?

2. Although the United States was also at war with Italy and Germany, Americans of Italian or German descent were not interned. Only Japanese-Americans were treated in this way. What reasons do you think might have been given for this inconsistency? Can you think of any other reasons that might not have been stated?

3. In what ways could the internment of Japanese-Americans be considered an irony, and an embarrassment to the administration?

GLOSSARY   **ancestry**—family background
   appellant—person appealing against court decisions
   curfew—order requiring people to stay in their homes after a certain hour

   espionage—spying
   sabotage—destruction of property by enemy agents

Sample Answers
Japanese-American Internment

A Basic Question: Can discrimination be legal?

1. The court upheld Hirabayashi's conviction, and maintained the constitutionality of Executive Order 9096, which authorized relocation.

2. The reasons given included:
   a) Japanese-Americans were concentrated in or near Portland, Seattle, and Los Angeles, large cities in an area deemed of military importance.
   b) For various reasons, Japanese-Americans had not been assimilated into society as a whole.
   c) Many Japanese children were sent to Japanese language schools, which were believed to be sources of Japanese nationalistic propaganda, cultivating allegiance to Japan.
   d) About 10,000 American-born children of Japanese parents were sent to Japan for part or all of their education.
   e) Many Japanese-Americans were not eligible for U.S. citizenship.
   f) Many Japanese-Americans were deemed, by Japanese law, to be citizens of Japan.
   g) Restrictions on privileges and opportunities for Japanese-Americans had increased their isolation, and their attachment to Japan.
   h) Anti-Japanese feeling after Pearl Harbor was so high that Japanese-Americans needed to be protected inside the camps.

   Students might suggest that racial prejudice in fact played a large part in the decision to relocate and intern Americans of Japanese descent.

3. While interning people of a specific race in this country, the administration was fighting to empty concentration camps in Europe. Also, many Japanese-Americans—some conscripted from internment camps—fought with distinction in the war.

For Further Reading

Armor, John, and Peter Wright. *Manzanar: Photographs by Ansel Adams; Commentary by John Hersey.* New York: Times Books, 1988.

Daniels, Roger. *Concentration Camps: North American Japanese in the United States and Canada During World War II.* Melbourne, FL: Krieger, 1981.

Grodzins, Morton. *Americans Betrayed.* Chicago: University of Chicago Press, 1974.

Irons, Peter. *Justice At War: The Inside Story of the Japanese-American Internment.* New York: Oxford University Press, 1984.

Myer, Dillon S. *Uprooted Americans: The Japanese Americans and the War Relocation Authority.* Tucson: University of Arizona Press, 1971.

Tateishi, John. *And Justice for All: An Oral History of the Japanese-American Detention Camps.* New York: Random House, 1984.

TenBroek, Jacobus, et al. *Prejudice, War and the Constitution: Causes and Consequences of the Evacuation of the Japanese Americans in World War II.* Berkeley: University of California Press, 1954.

Weglyn, Michi. *Years of Infamy: The Untold Story of America's Concentration Camps.* New York: Morrow, 1976.

1949—Truman's "Fair Deal"

Encouraged by his success in the 1948 elections, President Truman appeared before the 81st Congress to urge a comprehensive program of domestic reform.

. . . The Government has still other opportunities—to help raise the standard of living of our citizens. These opportunities lie in the fields of social security, health, education, housing, and civil rights.

The present coverage of the social security laws is altogether inadequate; the benefit payments are too low. One-third of our workers are not covered. . . .

We must spare no effort to raise the general level of health in this country. In a nation as rich as ours, it is a shocking fact that tens of millions lack adequate medical care. . . . Moreover, we need—and we must have without further delay—a system of pre-paid medical insurance which will enable every American to afford good medical care.

It is equally shocking that millions of our children are not receiving a good education. Millions of them are in overcrowded, obsolete buildings. We are short of teachers, because teachers' salaries are too low to attract new teachers, or to hold the ones we have. All these school problems will become much more acute as a result of the tremendous increase in the enrollment in our elementary schools in the next few years. . . .

The housing shortage continues to be acute. As an immediate step, the Congress should enact the provisions for low-rent public housing, slum clearance, farm housing, and housing research which I have constantly recommended. The number of low-rent public housing units provided for in the legislation should be increased to 1 million units in the next 7 years. . . . By producing too few rental units and too large a proportion of high-priced houses, the building industry is rapidly pricing itself out of the market. Building costs must be lowered. . . .

The driving force behind our progress is our faith in our democratic institutions. That faith is embodied in the promise of equal rights and equal opportunities which the founders of our Republic proclaimed to their countrymen and to the whole world. [President Truman's Annual State of the Union Message, January 5, 1949]

——Questions——

1. Name the problems Truman is trying to address in this excerpt. Were these problems recent developments? What causes contributed to these problems?

2. What steps can you think of to deal with some of these problems? What steps do you think have been taken?

3. Although Congress rejected many of Truman's proposed new laws, many were still passed. Which of the items included in the excerpt above do you think were the subjects of successful Fair Deal legislation?

4. Truman made this speech nearly half a century ago. Do these problems still exist, or has legislation been able to provide solutions to them?

GLOSSARY **embody**—represent, personify   **obsolete**—no longer useful

Sample Answers
Truman's "Fair Deal"

A Basic Question: Would it have been "fair"?

1. The problems named here include: inadequate Social Security coverage; poor health coverage; insufficient medical insurance; inadequate educational facilities; a shortage of housing. Many of these problems had been developing for years, and had been exacerbated by the Depression, as families lost all their savings, and farmers were forced to leave their farms and move to the cities.

2. Answers will vary. Many of these problems have been the subject of legislation several times in the decades since Truman's speech. The question of national medical insurance is currently much discussed, but no solution for this problem—or for many of the others Truman spoke about—had been found as of the early 1990's.

3. Congress approved legislation for: an expansion of Social Security benefits; the extension of rent controls; low-rental housing; and slum clearance programs. Other Fair Deal legislation included: increased federal expenditures for the Rural Electrification Administration, the Farmers Home Administration, and the Tennessee Valley Authority; increased FDIC coverage (to $10,000); increase in minimum wage for workers in interstate industries from 40 to 75 cents an hour; establishment of farm price supports; more IRS employees brought under civil service; expanded activities of the Reclamation Bureau in the development of flood control, hydroelectric plants, and irrigation projects.

4. Answers will vary. Students will probably answer that these issues remain problems today.

For Further Reading

Hamby, Alonzo L., ed. *Beyond the New Deal: Harry S. Truman and American Liberalism.* New York: Columbia University Press, 1973.

1951—The Korean War

In June, 1950, when North Korean troops moved across the border into South Korea, President Truman reacted quickly to contain the threat of communism. General Douglas MacArthur was named commander of U.N. troops in the area. But less than a year later, with Chinese troops involved and military lines stabilized near the North/South border, Truman contemplated negotiation. MacArthur, meanwhile, denounced limited war and called for an attack on China. In May, 1951, General Omar N. Bradley, Chairman of the Joint Chiefs of Staff, told the Senate why war with China should be avoided.

I am under no illusion that our present strategy of using means short of total war to achieve our ends and oppose communism is a guarantee that a world war will not be thrust upon us. But a policy of patience and determination without provoking a world war, while we improve our military power, is one which we believe we must continue to follow.

As long as we keep the conflict within its present scope, we are holding to a minimum the forces we must commit and tie down.

The strategic alternative, enlargement of the war in Korea to include Red China, would probably delight the Kremlin more than anything else we could do. It would necessarily tie down additional forces, especially our sea power and our air power, while the Soviet Union would not be obliged to put a single man into the conflict.

Under present circumstances, we have recommended against enlarging the war. The course of action often described as a "limited war" with Red China would increase the risk we are taking by enlarging too much of our power in an area that is not the critical strategic prize.

Red China is not the powerful nation seeking to dominate the world. Frankly, in the opinion of the Joint Chiefs of Staff, this strategy would involve us in the wrong war, at the wrong place, at the wrong time, and with the wrong enemy. [Gen. Omar N. Bradley at Senate hearings, May 15, 1951]

——Questions——

1. What arguments does General Bradley give against expanding the war in Korea?

2. What arguments do you think might have been given in favor of expanding the war?

3. The world political climate has changed drastically in the decades since the Korean War. Do you think this development would have been different if the U.S. had decided to pursue "total war" with China? Describe the world today as it might have been if we had gone to war with China in 1951.

Sample Answers
The Korean War

A Basic Question: Was MacArthur right?

1. a) We should try to maintain peace while we build up our military.
   b) Keeping the conflict small means we don't have to send in large numbers of troops.
   c) If we go to war with China, we actually make it easier for the Soviet Union to move elsewhere, because we'll be tied down in Korea.
   d) Any gains we might make against China would not be worth the increase in our risk.
   e) China isn't the big threat, Russia is. If we go to war with China, we're less likely to be able to fight Russia if that becomes necessary.

2. People who favored expanding the war in Korea, the so-called "Asia firsters," used several arguments. The main thrust of their position was that communism must be contained; no more nations must become communist, whether through revolution or conquest. With that as a given, they saw Red China as a constant threat. They argued that:

   a) The countries of the South and Southwest Pacific have limited military resources, and would need American assistance if attacked; as long as we control the seas and air in the Pacific, island nations are safe, because they cannot be attacked by ground troops.
   b) If we can stem the conflict in Korea, it will reassure other nations that we are able to protect them. Thus, they will not be tempted to ally themselves with communist forces as a means of securing their safety.
   c) If we do not stop the spread of communism now, in Korea, we will soon see more and more communist takeovers.
   d) The loss of southeast Asia to communism would jeopardize the security of the United States.
   e) Once southeast Asia fell to communism, Europe would be the next to go, as Russia would certainly turn its attention to the west as soon as it was secure in the east.

3. Answers will vary.

For Further Reading

Blair, Clay. *The Forgotten War: America in Korea, 1950-1953.* New York: Times Books, 1987.

Foot, Rosemary. *The Wrong War: American Policy and the Dimensions of the Korean Conflict, 1950-1953.* Ithaca: Cornell University Press, 1985.

Manchester, William. *American Caesar: Douglas MacArthur, 1880-1964.* Boston: Little, Brown, 1978.

Spanier, John W. *The Truman-MacArthur Controversy and the Korean War.* New York: Norton, 1965.

1954—McCarthyism

Early in 1950, Senator Joseph R. McCarthy of Wisconsin began a campaign to prove that the government was infested with communists and communist sympathizers. At various times, he charged that communist sympathizers had dictated American policy decisions and that such noted Americans as General George C. Marshall were communist dupes. Through clever manipulation of the media and evasion of demands for tangible proof, McCarthy developed a large following.

Over the course of the following four years, he led a witch-hunt for suspected communists in the federal government and elsewhere. Finally, in 1954, he took on the Army, but the televised Army-McCarthy hearings discredited him. That December the Senate voted to censure Senator McCarthy, and his influence declined. In this excerpt, Senator McCarthy was answering a question about receiving classified documents that he was not authorized to have.

I will continue to receive information. . . . That will be my policy. There's no power on earth can change that. Again, I want to compliment individuals [who] give me information even though some little bureaucrat has stamped it "secret" to defend himself. . . . None of them, none of them will be brought before a grand jury because of any information which I give. . . . I would like to notify two million federal employees that it is their duty to give us the information they have about graft, corruption, Communists, and treason, and that there is no loyalty to a superior officer that can tower above their loyalty to their country. . . . I just will not abide by any secrecy directive of anyone. [The Army-McCarthy hearings, 1954]

——Questions——

1. McCarthy's power and influence stemmed directly from his own personality. What does this excerpt tell you about the kind of man he was?

2. Was the post-World War II "red scare" unique in United States history? How can you account for this extraordinary period of panic and persecution?

3. McCarthy and his supporters argued that criticism of American institutions indicated disloyalty to the country. Opponents pointed out that laws directed against communists could also make it dangerous for others "to think, speak, or write critically." Which point of view would you support?

4. For about four years, McCarthy and his supporters made communism a divisive issue in U.S. politics. Name as many possible consequences of this government-sponsored campaign as you can think of.

GLOSSARY **bureaucrat**—employee who sticks firmly to rules and routines
directive—order

graft—using one's political position for dishonest gain

Sample Answers
McCarthyism

A Basic Question: Why was he so successful?

1. This excerpt makes it clear that McCarthy considered himself above the rules. While claiming to act in the interests of national security, he deliberately flouted national security precautions. If one carries McCarthy's arguments to their logical conclusion, everyone in government employment would have the right to ignore regulations—including those against hiring communists. He was also an adept manipulator, which we see here as he praises employees who have deliberately broken rules in order to supply him with material to which he should not have had access. McCarthy's description makes these individuals appear as small heroes. Some of them did doubtless act from the best motives—although these motives led them to break the rules of their own employment—but some undoubtedly acted in order to get revenge on colleagues. It was far easier to cry "Communist!" than to defend yourself against such a charge.

2. Throughout the nation's history, people have tended to reactionary responses in times of national crisis or war. The Alien and Sedition Acts of 1798, the anti-anarchist movement following World War I, and the internment of Japanese-Americans during World War II were all symptoms of the same kind of response. The years following World War II saw the development of the Cold War and the Korean War, and communist domination was seen as a real threat. In the light of that fear, many people saw nothing unreasonable in ferreting out communists wherever they were, and however far in the past their communist sympathies or involvements might have been.

3. Answers will vary.

4. Consequences include: national division; destruction of the careers of many innocent people; demoralization of federal workers, many of whom were driven from public service; people discouraged from expressing themselves freely, debating critical issues; contempt for the Bill of Rights.

For Further Reading

Caute, David. *The Great Fear: The Anti-Communist Purge Under Truman and Eisenhower.* New York: Simon and Schuster, 1978.

Ceplair, Larry and Steven Englund. *The Inquisition in Hollywood: Politics in the Film Community.* Berkeley: University of California Press, 1983.

Kutler, Stanley I. *The American Inquisition: Justice and Injustice in the Cold War.* New York: Hill & Wang, 1982.

Navasky, Victor. *Naming Names.* New York: Penguin, 1981.

Oshinsky, David M. *A Conspiracy So Immense: The World of Joe McCarthy.* New York: Free Press, 1983.

Reeves, Thomas C. *The Life and Times of Joe McCarthy.* Briarcliff Manor, NY: Stein & Day, 1981.

Rovere, Richard H. *Senator Joe McCarthy.* New York: Harper & Row, 1973.

1954—Segregation in Schools

In 1896, in a case known as *Plessy* v. *Ferguson,* the U.S. Supreme Court ruled that the terms of the Fourteenth Amendment had been met if blacks and whites had "separate but equal" accommodations. In 1954, Linda Brown was denied admission to an elementary school in Topeka because she was black. A suit was filed claiming that, despiite the earlier ruling, segregation was not constitutional. The case asked one basic question: Does the equal protection clause of the Fourteenth Amendment prohibit racial segregation in the public schools?

Chief Justice Warren. . . . In each of the cases, minors of the Negro race, through their legal representatives, seek the aid of the courts in obtaining admission to the public schools of their community on a non-segregated basis. In each instance, they have been denied admission to schools attended by white children under laws requiring or permitting segregation according to race. This segregation was alleged to deprive the plaintiffs of the equal protection of the laws under the Fourteenth Amendment. . . .

The plaintiffs contend that segregated public schools are not "equal" and cannot be made "equal," and that hence they are deprived of the equal protection of the laws. . . .

We conclude that in the field of public education the doctrine of "separate but equal" has no place. Separate educational facilities are inherently unequal. Therefore, we hold that the plaintiffs . . . are, by reason of the segregation complained of, deprived of the equal protection of the laws guaranteed by the Fourteenth Amendment. [*Brown* v. *Board of Education of Topeka,* 1954]

——Questions——

1. In *Plessy* v. *Ferguson,* the majority opinion was opposed by some judges. In this case, all the judges agreed with the opinion read by the Chief Justice. What, if any, is the significance of the unanimous opinion?

2. A lower court decided in favor of the Board of Education. Why do you think the Supreme Court reversed this ruling?

3. What effects do you think this decision has had on education in the United States?

4. What effects, if any, do you think this decision has had on other aspects of American life?

5. A year after this decision, the Court ordered the desegregation of schools "with all deliberate speed." How would you define "all deliberate speed"? How do you think the ambiguous wording of this order affected the speed with which it was carried out?

6. In this case, "separate but equal" referred to facilities for black and white Americans. Could the argument in the last paragraph of this excerpt be used against schools and colleges open only to men, or only to women?

GLOSSARY **facility**—something built to provide a service **inherently**—basically **minor**—person who has not yet reached legal age **nonsegregated**—not separated by race

Sample Answers
Segregation in Schools

A Basic Question: Can courts require integration?

1. Even when a majority of the Court agrees with a decision, there is often some dissent, or even a separate concurring opinion—one judge agrees with the verdict, but has some differences on the opinion itself. In this case, all the judges agreed. Chief Justice Earl Warren's opinion was very much "the opinion of the Court." All the judges, from North or South, conservatives and liberals, agreed that "in the field of public education, the doctrine of 'separate but equal' has no place." Such a unanimous opinion tends to indicate that the Court's opinion reflects the general feeling of society. A unanimous Court opinion certainly means that the Court is unlikely to reconsider or change its mind soon about the issue in question.

2. The lower court, although it felt compelled to rule against Linda Brown, stated its position on the effects of segregation:

Segregation of white and colored children in public schools has a detrimental effect upon the colored children. The impact is greater when it has the sanction of the law; for the policy of separating the races is usually interpreted as denoting the inferiority of the negro group. A sense of inferiority affects the motivation of a child to learn. Segregation with the sanction of law, therefore, has a tendency to [retard] the educational and mental development of negro children and to deprive them of some of the benefits they would receive in a racial[ly] integrated school system.

Taking these findings into account, the Supreme Court found that segregation is unequal by its very nature, and that therefore separate schools could not be equal.

3. The Brown decision has had considerable effect on education in America, but full desegregation of schools has not been achieved. The Supreme Court's mandate for "all deliberate speed" has received various checks. Particularly in the South, resistance to integration has been strong. Initially, integration even met outright defiance, as at Little Rock in 1958 and Oxford, Mississippi, in 1962, when federal troops were called in to enforce federal court decrees. New strategies, including magnet schools, are now being used in an effort to end segregation without resorting to unpopular methods like busing.

4. The decision in *Brown* v. *Board of Education* has become a landmark case in American constitutional law, and its influence has extended into many areas. Courts have used the Brown decision as a precedent to invalidate many other forms of state-enforced racial segregation, at public beaches, on municipal golf courses, on local buses, and in public parks and theaters. Indirectly, the decision in *Brown* v. *Board of Education* was the first great breakthrough for racial equality, and further gains in this area could hardly have been made without that first step.

5. The vagueness of this order encouraged southern states to resist complying with it. Some border states quietly put desegregation into effect, but many southern communities defied the Court's order. This resistance came to a head in 1957 in Little Rock, Arkansas, when a local plan for desegregation culminated in Eisenhower's decision to federalize the Arkansas National Guard and send paratroopers to Little Rock to ensure the safety of eight black high school students. Troops patrolled the school for the rest of the year, but in response, the Little Rock officials closed all public high schools in 1958 and 1959 rather than desegregate them.

6. Answers will vary.

For Further Reading

Eagles, Charles W., ed. *The Civil Rights Movement in America.* Jackson, MS: University Press of Mississippi, 1986.

Kluger, Richard. *Simple Justice: The History of* Brown *v.* Board of Education *and Black America's Struggle for Equality.* New York: Knopf, 1976.

McCord, John H., ed. *With All Deliberate Speed: Civil Rights Theory and Reality.* Champaign, IL: University of Illinois Press, 1969.

1958—Freedom of Association

The National Association for the Advancement of Colored People, or NAACP, was founded in 1909. It aimed to make sure that all African-Americans gained the rights they were guaranteed under the Constitution. The NAACP has been active in many areas, including the field of the law. In an effort to put an end to violations of constitutional rights, NAACP lawyers have brought many test cases before the courts. The best known of these is *Brown* v. *Board of Education,* which ended legal segregation in schools. In 1958, the NAACP appealed a decision of the Supreme Court of Alabama that had ended in a judgment of civil contempt against the NAACP because, in defiance of Alabama state law, the association had refused to give the state attorney general a list of all its members in Alabama. This excerpt is from the summing up and opinion:

Justice Harlan: . . . It is hardly a novel perception, that compelled disclosure of affiliation with groups engaged in advocacy may constitute as effective a restraint on freedom of association as the forms of governmental action in the cases above were thought likely to produce upon the particular constitutional rights there involved. This court has recognized the vital relationship between freedom to associate and privacy in one's associations. . . . Compelled disclosure of membership engaged in advocacy of particular beliefs is of the same order. Inviolability of privacy in group association may in many circumstances be indispensable for preservation of freedom of association, particularly where a group espouses dissident beliefs.

We think that the production order, in the respects here drawn in question, must be regarded as entailing the likelihood of a substantial restraint upon the exercise by petitioner's members of their right to freedom of association. Petitioner has made an uncontroverted showing that on past occasions revelation of the identity of its rank-and-file members has exposed those members to economic reprisal, loss of employment, threat of physical coercion, and other manifestations of public hostility. . . .
[*NAACP* v. *Alabama,* 1958]

——Questions——

1. Rewrite the last paragraph of this excerpt in your own words, trying to make the meaning as clear as possible.

2. Why do you think Alabama, and other southern states, enacted laws that required associations to give the attorney general full disclosure of membership, records, finances, and so forth?

3. Part of Alabama's argument in its favor was that the state itself was not responsible for the negative effects of disclosure, but that these effects came from private community pressures. How would you defend the NAACP's position against this argument?

GLOSSARY   **advocacy**—active support
coercion—force
constitute—make up
disclosure—making known
dissident—disagreeing
entail—involve
espouse—adopt an idea or cause

indispensable—essential
inviolability—indestructibility
novel—new
perception—insight
petitioner—person making a request
uncontroverted—undeniable

Sample Answers
Freedom of Association

A Basic Question: What is freedom of association?

1. Answers will vary. The general gist of the paragraph is: We think that ordering the NAACP to give the state a full list of all its members would probably affect the right those members have to join any groups they choose. The NAACP has shown very clearly the negative effects of naming members. People who were identified as members of the NAACP were harmed financially, they lost their jobs, they were threatened with physical force, and were made aware of public hostility in other ways.

2. The NAACP had made itself obnoxious to racist southern whites by spearheading the struggle for black rights in the South. Southern whites fought back against civil rights with laws harassing the NAACP. The law in question here could fall under that heading. If the NAACP gave out the names of its members, those people could be harassed as individuals. But if the association refused to comply with the disclosure order, it could be taken to court, as it was in Alabama.

3. Answers will vary. The court rejected this argument because "The crucial factor is the interplay of governmental and private action, for it is only after the initial exertion of state power represented by the production order that private action takes hold. . . ." In other words, NAACP members would not be harassed by members of the community unless their membership was revealed by the state's production order.

For Further Reading

Burk, Robert F. *The Eisenhower Administration and Black Civil Rights.* Knoxville: University of Tennessee Press, 1984.

Sitkoff, Harvard. *The Struggle for Black Equality, 1954-1980.* New York: Hill & Wang, 1981.

1966—The Rights of the Accused

In 1966, Ernesto Miranda appealed this case to the Supreme Court. Mr. Miranda had been arrested in Phoenix, Arizona, and interrogated by two police officers. The questioning took place in a special interrogation room. Mr. Miranda confessed orally to a charge of kidnapping and rape.

Chief Justice Warren: . . . The cases before us raise questions which go to the roots of our concept of American criminal jurisprudence: the restraints society must observe consistent with the Federal Constitution in prosecuting individuals for crime. More specifically, we deal with the admissibility of statements obtained from an individual who is subjected to custodial police interrogation and the necessity for procedures which assure that the individual is accorded his privilege under the Fifth Amendment to the Constitution not to be impelled to incriminate himself. . . .

We have concluded that without proper safeguards the process of in-custody interrogation of persons suspected or accused of crime contains inherently compelling pressures which work to undermine the individual's will to resist and that compel him to speak where he would not otherwise do so freely. In order to combat these pressures and to permit a full opportunity to exercise the privilege against self-incrimination, the accused must be adequately and effectively apprised of his rights and the exercise of those rights must be fully honored. [*Miranda v. Arizona,* 1966]

——Questions——

1. According to the Chief Justice, does this case address the question of Miranda's guilt or innocence of the crime to which he confessed?

2. In the last paragraph of this excerpt, the Chief Justice explains how the interrogation process, by its nature, can be prejudicial to the individual's rights. How do you think the accused could be "adequately and effectively apprised of his rights" in such a situation?

GLOSSARY **accord**—give
apprise—tell
custodial—in custody
incriminate—accuse of a crime
inherently—basically
interrogation—close questioning

jurisprudence—system of laws
privilege—right, benefit
procedure—way of doing something
self-incrimination—answering questions which might make one liable to criminal prosecution

Sample Answers
The Rights of the Accused

A Basic Question: What are the rights of the accused?

1. No. This case only addressed the question of Miranda's constitutional rights. Miranda had been found guilty of kidnapping and rape, and had been sentenced to prison for forty to fifty-five years. The Supreme Court ruling invalidated that trial. On the basis of new evidence, Miranda was later convicted again on the same charges, and imprisoned.

2. The opinion of the Chief Justice went on to state that: 1) If a person in custody is to be interrogated, that person must first be warned in clear terms that he or she has the right to remain silent, but that if the suspect does not choose to remain silent, anything the suspect says can be used as evidence against him or her. 2) The suspect must be informed that he or she has the right to have legal counsel present during an interrogation, and that if the suspect does not have an attorney, a lawyer will be appointed to represent him or her.

For Further Reading

Bickel, Alexander M. *The Supreme Court and the Idea of Progress.* New Haven: Yale University Press, 1978.

Galloway, John, ed. *The Supreme Court and the Rights of the Accused.* New York: Facts on File, 1973.

1973—Abortion

American abortion legislation began to be introduced during the nineteenth century. In 1840, only eight states had statutes dealing with abortion. By the end of the 1950's, most states allowed abortion only to save the mother's life. In January, 1973, the Supreme Court was asked to rule on two of these state statutes. One case, *Roe* v. *Wade,* was brought by an unmarried Texas woman. Texas abortion law made it a crime to "procure an abortion" unless the mother's life was in danger. In a 7-2 decision, the Court found that the Texas abortion statute, and others similarly worded, infringed on a woman's right to personal privacy. Justices White and Rehnquist filed a dissenting opinion:

At the heart of the controversy in these cases are those recurring pregnancies that pose no danger whatsoever to the life or health of the mother but are nevertheless unwanted for any one or more of a variety of reasons—convenience, family planning, economics, dislike of children, the embarrassment of illegitimacy, etc. . . . During the period prior to the time the fetus becomes viable, the Constitution of the United States values the convenience, whim or caprice of the putative mother more than the life or potential life of the fetus; the Constitution, therefore, guarantees the right to an abortion as against any state law or policy seeking to protect the fetus from an abortion not prompted by more compelling reasons of the mother.

With all due respect, I dissent. I find nothing in the language or history of the constitution to support the Court's judgment. The Court simply fashions and announces a new constitutional right for pregnant mothers and, with scarcely any reason or authority for its action, invests that right with sufficient substance to override most existing state abortion statutes. The upshot is that the people and the legislatures of the 50 States are constitutionally disentitled to weigh the relative importance of the continued existence and development of the fetus on the one hand against a spectrum of possible impacts on the mother on the other hand. As an exercise of raw judicial power, the Court perhaps has authority to do what it does today; but in my view its judgment is an improvident and extravagant exercise of the power of judicial review which the Constitution extends to this Court. [*Roe* v. *Wade*, 1973]

——Questions——

1. The majority of the Court agreed that a woman has a constitutional right to an abortion, subject to certain restrictions. You have read the dissenting opinion of two judges, Justices White and Rehnquist. What do you think the dissenting judges might have argued to support this opinion?

2. The usual rule of federal cases is that an actual controversy must exist at the time an appeal is brought, not just at the time when the action is begun. How would this affect a case involving pregnancy?

3. As the makeup of the Supreme Court changes, so does the Court's position on issues like abortion. What is the current status of abortion law?

GLOSSARY
caprice—impulsive change of mind
controversy—argument
disentitle—take away a right
fashion—make
illegitimacy—being born of unmarried parents
improvident—careless, not planning for the future

prior—before
spectrum—range, variety
statute—law
viable—able to live
whim—sudden desire

Sample Answers
Abortion

A Basic Question: Who has what rights?

1. The dissenting justices argued:

    a) As the actual controversy did not exist at the time the case was heard, there was no plaintiff capable of litigating the issue.

    b) The detailed restrictions that the Court placed on abortion were more appropriate to a legislative decision than to a judicial one.

    c) Since most states have had restrictions on abortions for at least a century, it would not seem that, as the Court stated, the right to an abortion was "so rooted in the traditions and conscience of our people as to be ranked as fundamental."

    d) The Court has had to stretch the scope of the Fourteenth Amendment to reach this decision.

    e) The drafters of the Fourteenth Amendment undoubtedly meant to leave the power to enact abortion laws with the individual states, which was the situation when this Amendment was drafted.

2. Since a normal pregnancy lasts 266 days, and the process of bringing a case to court and going through the appeals process can take years, the "actual controversy"—pregnancy—would never exist at the time a case came to the Supreme Court. Since this meant that pregnancy litigation could never be appealed, the Court decided to waive the "actual controversy" requirement in the case of pregnancy.

3. Answers will vary.

For Further Reading

Evans, Sara. *Personal Politics: The Roots of Women's Liberation in the Civil Rights Movement and the New Left.* New York: Random House, 1980.

Faux, Marian. Roe *v.* Wade: *The Story of the Landmark Supreme Court Decision that Made Abortion Legal.* New York: Dutton, 1989.

Luker, Kristin. *Abortion and the Politics of Motherhood.* Berkeley: University of California Press, 1984.

1973—Watergate

"Watergate" is the popular name for the political scandal that resulted in President Nixon's resignation in 1974. The scandal began with the arrest of five burglars in the Democratic National Committee headquarters at the Watergate building in Washington, D.C. The diligence and persistence of members of the press and of Judge John Sirica, the judge who tried the burglars, led to disclosures that seemed to link the burglary and other events to the White House. In April, 1973, President Nixon himself dealt with the subject in an address to the nation.

Good evening.

I want to talk to you tonight from my heart on a subject of deep concern to every American.

In recent months, members of my Administration and officials of the Committee for the Re-election of the President—including some of my closest friends and most trusted aides—have been charged with involvement in what has come to be known as the Watergate affair. . . .

The inevitable result of these charges has been to raise serious questions about the integrity of the White House itself. Tonight I wish to address those questions.

Last June 17, while I was in Florida trying to get a few days rest after my visit to Moscow, I first learned from news reports of the Watergate break-in. I was appalled at this senseless, illegal action, and I was shocked to learn that employees of the Re-election Committee were apparently among those guilty. I immediately ordered an investigation by appropriate Government authorities. On September 15, as you will recall, indictments were brought against seven defendants in the case.

As the investigation went forward, I repeatedly asked those conducting the investigation whether there was any reason to believe that members of my Administration were in any way involved. I received repeated assurances that there were not. . . .

Until March of this year, I remained convinced that the denials were true and that the charges of involvement by members of the White House Staff were false. . . . However, new information then came to me which persuaded me that there was a real possibility that some of these charges were true, and suggesting further that there had been an effort to conceal the facts both from the public, from you, and from me.

As a result, on March 21, I personally assumed the responsibility for coordinating intensive new inquiries into the matter, and I personally ordered those conducting the investigations to get all the facts and to report them directly to me, right here in this office.

I again ordered that all persons in the Government or at the Re-election Committee should cooperate fully with the FBI, the prosecutors, and the grand jury. I also ordered that anyone who refused to cooperate in telling the truth would be asked to resign from government service. And, with ground rules adopted that would preserve the basic constitutional separation of powers between the Congress and the Presidency, I directed that members of the White House Staff should appear and testify voluntarily under oath before the Senate committee which was investigating Watergate.

I was determined that we should get to the bottom of the matter, and that the truth should be fully brought out—no matter who was involved.

At the same time, I was determined not to take precipitate action, and to avoid, if at all possible, any action that would appear to reflect on innocent people. I wanted to be fair. But I knew that in the final analysis, the integrity of this office—public faith in the integrity of this office—would have to take priority over all personal considerations. . . .

(continued)

1973—Watergate
(continued)

I looked at my own calendar this morning up at Camp David as I was working on this speech. It showed exactly 1,361 days remaining in my term. I want these to be the best days in America's history, because I love America. I deeply believe that America is the hope of the world. And I know that in the quality and wisdom of the leadership America gives lies the only hope for millions of people all over the world, that they can live their lives in peace and freedom. We must be worthy of that hope, in every sense of the word. Tonight, I ask for your prayers to help me in everything that I do throughout the days of my Presidency to be worthy of their hopes and of yours.

God bless America and God bless each and every one of you. [Richard M. Nixon's Address to the Nation, April 30, 1973]

——Questions——

1. Hindsight—being able to see, after the event, what should have been done—can make many historical events seem very obvious. Our knowledge of Nixon's involvement in the Watergate scandal lets us see through this speech. But if, like much of the American public, you had not known of Nixon's guilt, how would you have reacted to this speech? Try to look at this speech with as few preconceptions as possible, and describe how it would have made you think about the president.

2. At many points in this speech, Nixon manipulates his audience. He distances himself from the Watergate scandal, stressing his hard work, his devotion to duty, and his patriotism. List as many of these points as you can.

3. Rewrite all or part of this speech as Nixon might have written it if he were telling the truth.

4. A cynic is defined as "a person who believes that people are motivated in all their actions entirely by selfishness." The Watergate scandal brought a cynical reaction from many people. Why do you think it may have had this effect?

GLOSSARY   **indictment**—accusation of crime   **precipitate**—hasty, impulsive

Sample Answers
Watergate

A Basic Question: What did the president know?

1. Answers will vary, depending on how objectively students are able to read the excerpt. Some students may feel that this is a very persuasive speech. The president's apparent frankness and sense of personal outrage would go a long way towards allaying fears of his complicity.

2. Answers will vary. Almost every paragraph contains lines indicative of expert manipulation, from the second paragraph, which links Nixon with his innocent, concerned audience, to the emotional closing words.

3. Answers will vary. Rewriting efforts may produce paragraphs like: Last June 17, while I was in Florida resting up after a well-publicized junket, I first learned from news reports that the Plumbers had bungled their break-in, and had been arrested. I was appalled that they were so unprofessional about doing something illegal, and hoped that no one would put two and two together to link me up with my campaign employees. I immediately ordered a cover-up. On September 15, as you will recall, indictments were brought against seven defendants in the case, but they were well primed to keep their mouths shut.

4. One of Nixon's arguments in his defense was that what he did wasn't really any worse than what other people, even other presidents, had done. The only difference was that other presidents had not been caught, while Nixon was brought down by a vindictive press. Many people were convinced that what Nixon did was normal for the presidency. Opinion polls taken during the crisis made this clear. While a majority said they believed that Nixon was lying about Watergate, four out of five thought he was no more corrupt than his predecessors. On the eve of his resignation, one out of two wanted the Senate to impeach Nixon, but only one out of four thought it would.

For Further Reading

Bernstein, Carl, and Bob Woodward. *All the President's Men.* New York: Warner Books, 1976.

Kurland, Philip B. *Watergate and the Constitution.* Chicago: University of Chicago Press, 1978.

Lukas, J. Anthony. *Nightmare: The Underside of the Nixon Years.* New York: Viking, 1976.

Schell, Jonathan. *The Time of Illusion.* New York: Knopf, 1976.

Sirica, John. *To Set the Record Straight: The Break-In, the Tapes, the Conspirators, the Pardon.* New York: New American Library, 1980.

White, Theodore H. *Breach of Faith: The Fall of Richard Nixon.* New York: Dell, 1986.

1982—The Equal Rights Amendment

The Equal Rights Amendment, or ERA, was first proposed in 1923. The amendment was intended to outlaw discrimination based on sex, and stated that "equality of rights under the law shall not be denied or abridged by the United States nor by any State on account of sex." The ERA lay dormant until 1970, when a groundswell of support was generated by the National Organization for Women (NOW). The ERA was approved by the House of Representatives in 1971 and by the Senate in 1972. The deadline for ratification by at least thirty-eight states was originally March 1979, but it was extended to June 30, 1982. By that date, only thirty-five of the required thirty-eight states had ratified the amendment.

On June 24, 1982, Eleanor Smeal, then president of the National Organization for Women, issued a statement announcing the end of the campaign to pass the Equal Rights Amendment.

We are announcing today that the Equal Rights Amendment (ERA) Countdown Campaign, coordinated by the National Organization for Women, has ended. However, the fight for equality for women will go on, stronger than ever, until justice is ours.

In this long and intensive fight for the ERA, a number of political realities have emerged which must be changed before ratification can be achieved.

1. The Republican Party has not only deserted women's rights, it has actually led the attack against them. In both Oklahoma and North Carolina, Republicans bloc-voted against the Amendment, and overall, 83% of Republicans in unratified states opposed it.

2. While the Democrats provided words of encouragement, and undeniably supported the ERA in greater numbers than Republicans, that support was not strong enough, and lacked the political cohesiveness to achieve victory. In short, women's rights were not high on their agenda and there was significant defection in their ranks. . . .

3. The real opposition, behind the visible political opposition . . . has been the special corporate interests that profit from sex discrimination. . . .

4. Another major source of ERA opposition has been, simply, sex bias in the legislatures. In those legislative bodies, women have had token representation at best. . . . The preponderance of men in the legislatures has created a "stag club" atmosphere which keeps those bodies from being representative of women or responsive to women's concerns. [Statement by Eleanor Smeal, president of NOW, June 24, 1982]

——Questions——

1. Ms. Smeal states that corporations "profit from sex discrimination." How do you think large companies might profit from discriminating against women?

2. The proposed amendment was controversial, with formidable conservative opposition. What arguments do you think the opponents of the ERA may have used?

3. What arguments do you think supporters of the ERA may have used?

4. Although the Equal Rights Amendment was not passed, it has had some effects on legislation. What kind of effects do you think the failed amendment might have had?

GLOSSARY   cohesiveness—sticking together   ratification—official approval
                    defection—deserting

Sample Answers
The Equal Rights Amendment

A Basic Question: Who is against equal rights for women?

1. Many companies consistently pay women less for the same work as men. Thus, a company that hires a talented, qualified woman, instead of an equally well-qualified man, can often get the same skills for thousands of dollars less a year.

2. The opposition to the ERA reflected three distinct views:
   1) that inequality between men and women is biologically and psychologically determined and cannot be changed;
   2) that the ERA would have an adverse impact on social institutions such as marriage, the family, morality, child care, and the economic benefits women derive from their dependence on men; and
   3) that an amendment is neither necessary nor proper, since discriminatory practices could be changed at the state level or by appeal to the Supreme Court on the grounds of the Fifth and Fourteenth Amendments.

3. ERA's supporters contend that it is a needed extension of the equal protection clause of the Fourteenth Amendment, making the constitutional attitude toward sex discrimination explicit, rather than implicit, and therefore debatable. The objective is to place such discrimination within the direct context of violation of constitutional rights, the most serious sanction in the U.S. legal system.

4. Between 1972 and 1979, sixteen states adopted ERA amendments for their own constitutions.

For Further Reading

Berry, Mary Frances. *Why ERA Failed: Politics, Women's Rights, and the Amending Process of the Constitution.* Bloomington: Indiana University Press, 1986.

Dworkin, Andrea. *Right-Wing Women: The Politics of Domesticated Females.* New York: Putnam Publishing Group, 1983.

Hoff-Wilson, Joan. *Law, Gender, and Injustice: A Legal History of U.S. Women.* New York: New York University Press, 1990.

Mansbridge, Jane. *Why We Lost the ERA.* Chicago: University of Chicago Press, 1986.

Rhode, Deborah. *Justice and Gender: Sex Discrimination and the Law.* Cambridge: Harvard University Press, 1989.

1991—Women in Combat

During the 1991 war in the Persian Gulf, 35,000 women took part in Operation Desert Storm. Eleven of these women were killed, five due to hostile action, six due to accidents or natural causes. Two women were taken prisoner by the Iraqis. But despite the active part they play in the armed forces, American women are not allowed to take part in active combat. In July 1991, the question of women in combat was debated in the Senate; senators decided to repeal a 1948 law barring the assignment of women to air warfare, and to set up a commission to study the issues involved in assigning women to combat. Senator Edward Kennedy spoke to the Senate in favor of repealing the 1948 law:

. . . The Armed Forces claim that they are an equal opportunity employer, and they are, partly. They have made great strides in opening up all branches of the service to racial minorities.

But the same cannot be said with regard to sex discrimination, because archaic statutes still in the books deny equal opportunity to women.

Barriers based on sex discrimination are coming down in every part of our society. The Armed Forces should be no exception. Women should be allowed to play a full role in our national defense, free of any arbitrary and discriminating restrictions. The only fair and proper test of a woman's role is not gender but ability to do the job. . . .

The dangers [of war] now extend well behind the front lines. As we saw in the Persian Gulf War, military personnel well behind the lines can be killed or wounded. At the same time, the infusion of advanced electronic and computer technology into modern weapons has changed many phases of warfare from a test of physical strength to a test of technical skill.

In the gulf war, the technological abilities of our personnel were as important to our victory as their physical strength and courage. There is virtually universal consensus that the women who served in Operation Desert Storm did an outstanding job, including jobs that were, for all practical purposes, combat jobs. They faced hostile fire; they flew into enemy territory; they suffered death, injury, and were captured as prisoners of war; they lived in conditions of extreme hardship, and they performed tasks requiring physical strength and stamina.

In short, to quote Secretary of Defense Dick Cheney, women members of our armed forces "were every bit as professional as their male colleagues." [Remarks by Sen. Edward Kennedy in the Senate, July 31, 1991]

——Questions——

1. The repeal of the 1948 law means that the Air Force may, if it wishes, assign women to fly into combat; it doesn't mean that women *must* be given combat assignments. What questions do you think the commission studying the effects of assigning women to combat will try to address?

2. List as many arguments as you can think of both for and against opening combat assignments to women.

3. In assigning fitness ratings, the armed forces use a procedure called "gender norming" to ensure that positions are filled with a gender-balanced mix. Under gender norming, women are given less physically challenging tests than men to attain the same fitness rating. If combat positions are opened to women, do you think gender-norming should be continued?

GLOSSARY   arbitrary—based on impulse, not on reason   consensus—general agreement
archaic—not current, antiquated

Sample Answers

Women in Combat

A Basic Question: Should women fight?

1. Answers will vary. Senator Glenn, one of the sponsors of the amendment calling for the commission, included these questions as ones which must be answered before women are assigned to combat positions:

   a) If combat assignments are open to women, should assignment of women to these positions be voluntary? Or should women be compelled to serve in combat assignments regardless of their personal desires in the same manner that men can be assigned involuntarily to combat positions?

   b) Should women be required to register, and be subject to the draft on the same basis as men, if women are to have the same opportunity as men to compete for all skills and positions in the military? If current combat exclusion laws are repealed, but the military services retain the discretion to prescribe combat assignment restrictions for women, what effect will this have on the constitutionality of male-only registration and service requirements of the Military Selective Service Act?

   c) What are the physical requirements for each combat skill or position, including the full implications of gender norming? What are the full implications of gender norming where there are physical requirements and men and women are treated alike?

   d) What is the impact of pregnancy and child care on assignment policies for military personnel?

   e) What practical effect does opening combat skills and positions to women have on unit morale and cohesion?

   f) What would be the impact of required changes in quarters, weapons, training, and the resultant costs of changes?

   g) What would be the practical rate at which any required changes can be made in an era of severely constrained defense budgets?

2. Answers will vary. Arguments may include:
   In favor of opening combat positions to women:

   a) Women need combat experience to get top jobs in the military. The current prohibition limits their career prospects.

   b) Women have proven themselves in battle conditions in the Persian Gulf.

   c) The armed forces should assign personnel based on ability, not gender.

   d) Technological developments have reduced many of the demands for physical strength in military personnel.

   e) Front-line forces are no longer the only ones at risk. Women already share the risks of war; let them share the responsibilities and rewards, as well.

   f) During the Gulf War, pregnancies accounted for a smaller number of casualties than men's sports injuries; the possibility of pregnancy is no hindrance to a woman's being a good soldier.

Against opening combat positions to women:

a) Women can't handle the stress of killing an enemy face to face.

b) Men will be overprotective of women in a combat unit, and may jeopardize an entire mission to ensure a woman's safety.

c) Including women in combat units would interfere with the "male bonding" that helps a group of men perform as a unit.

d) Pregnancy could lead to breaking up units on the verge of combat.

e) It's a waste of money to spend millions training women for specialized positions, only to have them get pregnant and be unable to fill those positions.

f) While women officers are eager to improve their career prospects, many enlisted women don't want to go into combat.

g) Women couldn't endure the savagery of ground combat.

h) Women are already represented in 97 percent of military job assignments; it isn't discriminating to keep them out of that last 3 percent.

i) Women aren't strong enough to fight in combat. Army studies show that only 18 percent of women recruits can lift between 50 and 100 pounds; a foot-soldier's rifle, ammunition, and gear average 110 pounds.

j) The military has seen enough experimentation for the moment. We shouldn't put women into combat before we know more about the effects this will have.

k) In combat conditions, it is impossible to provide enough privacy to have mixed-gender units.

l) The cost of renovating ship's quarters, etc., to accommodate mixed-gender units would be prohibitive.

3. Answers will vary.

For Further Reading

Holm, Jeanne. *Women in the Military: An Unfinished Revolution.* Rev. ed. Novato, CA: Presidio Press, 1992.

Wekesser, Carol and Matt Polesetsky, eds. *Women in the Military.* St. Paul, MN: Greenhaven Press, 1991.

1991—Clarence Thomas Confirmation Hearings

In the summer of 1991, President Bush nominated Clarence Thomas to the Supreme Court. In early October, just days before the Senate was due to vote on the nomination, a scandal broke. Anita Hill, one of Thomas's former aides, claimed that he had sexually harassed her from 1981 to 1983, while she worked for him. Both Hill and Thomas testified before the Senate Judiciary Committee.

Anita Hill: . . . After approximately three months of working there, he asked me to go out socially with him. . . . I thought that by saying no and explaining my reasons, my employer would abandon his social suggestions. However, to my regret, in the following few weeks, he continued to ask me out on several occasions. . . .

My working relationship became even more strained when Judge Thomas began to use work situations to discuss sex. . . . After a brief discussion of work, he would turn the conversation to a discussion of sexual matters. His conversations were very vivid. He spoke about acts that he had seen in pornographic films. . . . On several occasions, Thomas told me graphically of his own sexual prowess.

Because I was extremely uncomfortable talking about sex with him at all, and particularly in such a graphic way, I told him that I did not want to talk about this subject. I would also try to change the subject to educational matters or to nonsexual personal matters, such as his background or his beliefs.

My efforts to change the subject were rarely successful.

Clarence Thomas: . . . I have been racking my brains and eating my insides out trying to think of what I could have said or done to Anita Hill to lead her to allege that I was interested in her in more than a professional way, and that I talked with her about pornographic or X-rated films. . . .

Our relationship remained both cordial and professional. At no time did I become aware, either directly or indirectly, that she felt I had said or done anything to change the cordial nature of our relationship. . . . I had no reason or basis to believe that my relationship with Anita Hill was anything but this way until the F.B.I. visited me a little more than two weeks ago. [Testimony of Anita Hill and Clarence Thomas before Senate Judiciary Committee, Oct. 11, 1991]

——Questions——

1. Anita Hill claimed that the events she described took place almost ten years before Judge Thomas's nomination to the Supreme Court. What do you think may have been her reasons for reporting them when she did?

2. Some of Thomas's supporters pointed out that Anita Hill voluntarily stayed in a job where she claimed to be harassed. How do you think Hill might have answered that argument?

3. Judge Thomas refused to watch or listen to Anita Hill's testimony before the Senate Judiciary Committee. As a member of the committee, how would you have reacted to learning this?

(continued)

1991—Clarence Thomas Confirmation Hearings

(continued)

——Questions——

4. The Senate did not have to decide whether or not Hill's allegations were true, merely whether—in the light of these charges—they wished to confirm Thomas's nomination. If you had been a member of the Senate, how would you have voted?

GLOSSARY **cordial**—friendly, pleasant
graphic—described in vivid detail

prowess—power, ability

Sample Answers
Clarence Thomas Confirmation Hearings

A Basic Question: Was justice served?

1. Answers will depend on whether students believe Hill was lying or telling the truth. Hill herself claimed that she only spoke out because she felt Thomas's actions raised questions about his fitness to serve on the Supreme Court: "I believe that his conduct reflects his sense of how to carry out his job, and that, in effect, he did not feel himself compelled to comply with the guidelines that were established by the E.E.O.C." while he himself was the chairman of the Equal Employment Opportunity Commission.

2. Answers will vary. One reason Hill gave was that she was afraid she would lose her job if she complained. Experts on sexual harassment described Hill's allegations as "a model for some of the sexual harassment cases that have gone to the Federal courts over the last decade." Since most sexual harassment is not witnessed by other people, it cannot be corroborated. Victims fear that they will not be believed, or even that people will say the victim was "asking for it," that the harassment would not have continued if the victim had not, in fact, enjoyed it. Another reason many victims of sexual harassment do not report it is that sexual harassment, legally speaking, is a relatively new idea. Harassment on the job only came to be viewed as discrimination in the late 1970's. In 1986, the Supreme Court ruled that sexual harassment was a form of sex discrimination under Title VII of the Civil Rights Act of 1964. Until then, there were few clear legal guidelines for either employees or employers. With recent media attention on sexual harassment—especially since the Thomas hearings—many women and men are coming forward with reports of sexual harassment at work.

3. Answers will vary. Judge Thomas described his refusal to watch Hill's testimony by saying that he had heard enough lies, and wouldn't listen to any more. Some senators were baffled by his refusal to listen to the testimony so that he could rebut it. To some, this showed a closed mind and raised "issues of judicial temperament."

4. Answers will vary. The Senate confirmed Judge Thomas's nomination.

For Further Reading

Phelps, Timothy M., and Helen Winternitz. *Capitol Games: Clarence Thomas, Anita Hill, and the Behind-the-Scenes Story of a Supreme Court Nomination.* New York: Hyperion, 1992.

Morrison, Toni, ed. *Race-ing Justice, En-gendering Power: Essays on Anita Hill, Clarence Thomas and the Construction of Social Reality.* New York: Pantheon, 1992.